To Marvin Victor
In appreciation of your many contributions, thanks

STAN

Joe Norwood's Golf-o-Metrics

With Marilynn Smith and Stanley Blicker

Illustrations by George Janes

DOUBLEDAY & COMPANY, INC.
GARDEN CITY, NEW YORK
1978

Library of Congress Cataloging in Publication Data

Norwood, Joe.
  Joe Norwood's Golf-o-metrics.

  1. Swing (Golf). 2. Golf. I. Smith, Marilynn,
joint author. II. Blicker, Stanley, joint author.
III. Title. IV. Title: Golf-o-metrics.
GV979.S9N67 1978   796.352'3
ISBN: 0-385-01823-1
Library of Congress Catalog Card Number 75–21238

Contents

Introducing Joe Norwood

Hyperbole, an exaggeration of a point at issue. When one begins to talk of Joe Norwood's golf swing, it must necessarily sound like hyperbole. The purity of truth in his teachings cannot be denied and can prove each and every point many ways through his vast knowledge of the anatomy as it relates to the golf swing.

There is no doubt that Joe Norwood, in terms of golf, invented the printing press, invented paper and ink, then proceeded to create the bible of golf. He has spent many, many years in researching the elusive parts of the golf swing. Over sixty-five years of teaching. In his youth he met men many years his senior who already had long years of teaching experience. In those days they were either from Scotland or England. So he has well over a hundred years of accumulated knowledge at this point in time. He learned all of the terms commonly used in teaching, and being dissatisfied, he "found the parts of the body to fit the terms." To say that he has a blueprint for the golf swing is to invite controversy, yet give Joe six to eight minutes and anyone will admit that it is a fact.

He is a lover of baseball—of all sports, for that matter—and a great student of form. His basics are valid in every sport, and his keen eye isolated the "how to" that went into each sport. He sets up a tremendous left arm and of course can only hit a ball perfectly straight each and every time. It is a great privilege to watch Joe hit a few golf balls now and then. He swings to and from his Position One absolutely without any effort. He does have a blueprint for the swing, after all.

He is an amazing person, over eighty years of age and teaching full time. He is as full of zest at the end of a day as he is with the first lesson of the day. The last student receives as much attention as the first, and more than likely Joe will squander far more time on those still around after practice sessions than for the time he is paid.

He is qualified to hang three shingles above the golf shop. He is a master teacher, psychiatrist, and chiropractor. Since he is a charter member of the Southern California PGA and a golf professional, he merely is an amateur at the other skills. He was attached to the Los Angeles Country Club for twenty-five years. The very first Los Angeles Open was held there and directed by Joe.

Joe played golf with many of the famous early golfers—Francis Ouimet and Walter J. Travis, to start with. It was in 1913 that Joe met and played with the still-famous Walter J. Travis. Joe's all-time favorite professional was Walter Hagen. Hagen had every shot in the bag according to Joe, and the Haig would walk into a locker room and ask those present "who would be coming in second in the tournament."

In the early part of his career he worked for the Wright & Ditson Company. He serviced about ninety pros, and in those days he hefted clubs by hand in order to assemble a matched set. He has huge hands and to this day has the touch and feel of a fine surgeon. He has a correspondingly advanced knowledge of anatomy as it relates to golf. He is more privileged to teach knowing anatomy as he does.

To paraphrase Joe when he relates what one old-time pro way back in 1911 said to him in trying to teach him how to teach, "Tell them anything, they won't know the difference. When you finish your three weeks with me you will be the first pro to teach pros how to teach." There seems to be a vast number of convenient phrases that seem to fit a great number of errors, valid or not, still in use today.

Golf is still taught as it was before Joe was born. His greatest desire is to see the PGA adopt a uniform method of teaching instead of the individual theories confusing the public.

In a matter of minutes Joe never fails to get an exciting response out of a student. "Mr. Magic" . . . every few minutes someone is getting a thrill from a new sensation. "When you come to Joe, just bring your arms and legs, leave your body at home" is standard instruction to one and all. He is prone to say, "Take the mystery out of the swing, keep it simple." He subtracts from what the pupil brings to him and of course starts by reducing the greatest error first.

Joe has several patents on some really great mechanical aids that give one an immediate feel of what takes place in the action of the swing. One in particular is fifty years old. He is the proverbial bottomless well. There seems to be no end of information he has about what goes into the golf swing or how a shot should be made. He is just about as alert today regarding new ideas about golf as he ever was, and he is still searching.

He permits no one the luxury of indulging in negativity, and he believes in self-confidence, but he feels you had better have a good golf swing and not rely too much on confidence. No one dares to say "can't." He scolds them and tells them to say, "I took it out of use" instead.

He gives you the mechanics to work with. He wishes he could rent out his feelings or put them in pill form. He is apt to chide someone with the observation, "If it was so simple to teach I would need a staff of thirty secretaries and an office on Wilshire Boulevard to handle all of the customers." Usually this is directed to a dejected player.

First and foremost, Joe is a giver of himself. He was content to dedicate himself to being a teacher. Money has to be forced upon him when lesson time is over. He never fails to look you over for errors when you are there for a practice session and oftentimes spends a considerable amount of time doing so, *gratis*.

Joe always validates people. He always gives them something to tie to and leaves them with a great confident feeling. An opportunity to teach is a challenge, and Joe always responds.

—Stanley Blicker

The Premise

A golf swing that can be repeated consistently.

Being able to hit a ball straight on purpose. This includes every shot from a drive to a putt.

Almost everyone can tell you what to do, but Joe Norwood can tell you and show you how it is done, not theoretically, but physically.

Not what to do, but how to, and what to do it with.

Facts

The same grip is used with all clubs and for all shots. This means from a drive to a putt.

All the parts to be disciplined and all the moves to be made are the same in all shots.

There are no contradictions, and only one exception, in the Joe Norwood golf swing. The exception is the lob, or cut shot, or the pizza, as Joe Norwood likes to call it.

There are four major parts in the Joe Norwood golf swing:

> The right leg
> The left arm
> The right arm
> The left leg

There are four "positions" or sequences in the swing, called simply Position One, Position Two, Position Three, and Position Four.

And there are but four bywords, in this order:

> Knowledge
> Application
> Feel
> Judgment

Observations and Alternatives

The universal method of teaching usually goes like this: Keep your head still, go straight back from the ball, get the hips out of the way, pull down with the left, wait for the clubhead, turn the hands over, etc., *ad infinitum*. The mind isn't receptive to that many commands. One gets a headache trying to remember all of this during a golf swing. There is too much theory instead of fact brought to a point of analysis. Golf is 10 per cent fact and 90 per cent conversation.

Teaching the negative is not necessary, since the average person is already well equipped with that attribute as far as the mechanics of the swing is concerned. The negatives of golf never, but never, leave you. They are always there to haunt you. What allows you to hit the ball must be substituted for the built-in negatives. To repeat: Error is always waiting for you, it never leaves; therefore the need for discipline and knowledge to make the correct moves at all times.

Lifting muscles, swinging muscles, pulling muscles, throwing muscles, pushing muscles—these are all closely related. To boil or to bake a potato? One way takes about twenty minutes and the other about an hour. Application of dry heat or wet heat for whatever ache or pain? Both of these are useful and yet require a choice and can be right or wrong in their use. Fortunately for the golfer there are only two ways to swing the club, and those are by either pulling or pushing. It is that simple, and therein lies the major difference twixt Joe and the other experts. The majority pull to swing and this is a rotating action and the untrained legs take the line of least resistance and complete the rotation of the golfer. Rotating is easy to do. The body is accustomed to it and responds readily. It is such a natural action. Why then are there such few good golfers? If rotating is so great, why is it so hard to hit a ball straight on purpose? Rotating and pulling really are not the best ways to make a golf swing.

Compare a sliding door on a track with an ordinary door operating on a well-oiled hinge. To move the sliding door requires effort from the arms, body, legs, and even a heave-ho. The other example can be operated with the touch of a finger. Open and close a swinging door fast and watch the leading edge of the door. Note the tremendous speed and arc of the leading edge. Note how effortless it is to activate the door. The arc is a half circle going and coming, and so is Joe's golf swing. Tremendous centrifugal force is being generated. The sliding door has none of these good features—just the opposite, in fact. The arc of the swinging door is constant, and there is no change in the dimension from the hinge to the leading edge. The golf swing should travel in the same manner. Joe's blueprint for the golf swing has a hub, a constant radius; it generates centrifugal force with very little effort, it repeats itself continuously, and it is dependable. Unfortunately, most golfers break the arc in trying to go to the ball, hitting from the top, swinging around the hips instead of under the hips. Joe's swing is two half circles, and one must come down on the same track as the backswing takes going up.

Emphasize this thought: In all shots from a drive to a putt, hold the left arm and smack it with the right arm. Snatching at the club will only result in wild variations of swing patterns and will not lead to building a repeating golf swing. Swing with the arms and leave the body out of it.

Great emphasis must be made about the horizontal vs. the vertical. Most players start the downswing with a pull from the left shoulder instead of going down with the right shoulder. The left shoulder initiates the move and is followed by a snatch with the left elbow/forearm/hand. Or they start with a lunge of the right shoulder toward the ball and cast from the right hand. What did I do wrong? It is a miserable situation not knowing the reasons for such well-intended actions.

To eliminate error, one needs a substitute. The concert pianist has full command of the keyboard. He learned his basics from a musical scale, not by ear. The pianist is always reminiscing with the positive, or the scales, if you please. Most golfers "play by ear": They never did learn the basics involved simply because no valid ones were ever really offered to them. They spend most of their time reminiscing with the negative in a trial-and-error process.

Repetition of error is not experience, nor is it a substitute for a positive. "What did I do wrong" is added repetition of the negative. It doesn't add to what should be done right. Forget "What did I do wrong?" and eliminate it from the thought process completely.

It is interesting to watch the golfers on a driving range. One sees so many angles, patterns, planes, or tracks in the execution of the swing, so many wavelengths on the backswing and as many on the downswing. Angles produce a bad golf swing, but what produces the angles? One must change the idiosyncrasies that produce the erratic wavelengths into moves that can be repeated continuously in the exactness of a blueprint being reproduced by a copying machine.

Joe Norwood has isolated the parts of the golf swing. Everyone is familiar

Action of the arms in the Norwood arc. Place the left hand on the shaft at the clubhead with the left arm straight. Now place the right thumb and forefinger on the end of the handle, swinging to Position One. The right hand and wrist cocked. The right forearm and elbow parallel to the ground.

Now retain the right-hand and wrist-cock position while you lower by pushing, not pulling, the right hand and arm downward in a vertical position.

The right hand and arm continue to straighten
to the position opposite the right knee.

The right hand and wrist at no time separate
from the right arm while pushing against the
left arm, knee, and foot in a crosslateral
position, going outward and upward, taking
the right shoulder, hip, and knee under,
producing a high finish.

with a ratchet wrench. Joe found the circle of his golf swing by the use of a ratchet-type move that he developed as an enlargement of the putting stroke, and this went into every swing regardless of the club being used.

Golf requires fluidness and speed, not strength. There is no real power in the golf swing, just speed. Joe's golf-o-metrics—over one hundred movements and position exercises—are designed to give a uniform feeling of a swing. He teaches the cause and not the effect. Without the golf-o-metrics it is at best a vague and uncertain science, or art form. By guess and by gosh is about par for the individualized teaching available to the public. There are too many variations in the individuals, too many variations in the teaching, and it all becomes compounded and leads to much confusion. To eliminate error, both must be reduced.

There is a time element involved. There is a learning curve. There is no shortcut to acquiring the knowledge and the application of it, other than practicing the "scales," and in this case that means Joe's golf-o-metrics. This will provide you with an ever-developing sense of feel and the ability to recover your swing at all times.

Feelings come and go, and at best they are fleeting from hole to hole and day to day. Learning the parts and moves of the swing gives one something to tie to, something that can become disciplined, something the golfer can own, something to build a swing on and reduce the mystery of the swing to known facts. Errors are encouraged by the anxiety to hit the ball. The desire to go to the ball is lessened due to a growing trust in making the moves. Reminiscing with the keyboard builds and strengthens the good habits so necessary in overcoming the built-in error factors.

There is no way an artist can become a good craftsman without having studied the anatomy and knowing it cold. Artists introduce dynamic tension in their work by altering a straight line, a curve, or an angle. The golfer must learn what parts are to be used and how to set them dynamically.

A top-notch pro shot a sixty-seven and topped it off with a supersharp practice session, leaving the pro happy in the knowledge that he finally, at long last, had locked his swing in place. His first tee shot the next day hooked into some trees and left a most bewildered pro searching for his feelings as the next shot and the next shot went astray. His locked-in swing was gone, and so were his feelings. It seems they evaporated with the experience of the first hole. Gone was that superconfident feeling of the night before, and what could he attach to in order to recover his feelings? He had learned his swing through trial and error based purely on feelings. Unfortunately, he didn't have the counterpart of a musical scale. No real checkpoints to refer to, just vague feelings now. Words will not substitute for action. Therefore, the golf-o-metrics are needed to provide dependable feelings and checkpoints. Discipline the parts as needed to suit the action, and then they will work for you. Once you own them they will in great part work for you almost automatically. Put a premium on your feelings when they are based on the checkpoints of the golf-o-metrics. When you reach this stage of feeling you can stop thinking and think of judgment only as you will own the other element, which is line, the flight of the ball on a straight line. Get feelings through muscular movements afforded by the golf-o-metrics.

Miss the shot in the hunt for feelings. Waste a lot of shots in the search. It is better than pulling, hooking, and slicing. Joe's swing will put you on a dependable track eventually, whereas the variations of an undisciplined swing will never leave you.

Joe has the only swing that permits returning the club to the ball to the address position after a full swing without resetting the hands/wrists or the need to realign the face of the club. Joe never changes the position of the blade during the swing, whereas the loose left wrist and the oscillating motions of the right hand will necessitate resetting of the blade.

(Instructions and references to motions in this book are always given in terms of the right-handed golfer.)

Almost all golfers are left-sided golfers. The player remains on his left side at the address position and never makes an actual weight shift to his right side. On the downswing he tries to shift to his left side, and being already on it, he has no place to go and wonders why he can't get his right side into the shot. Most golfers cannot lift their left leg when they are at the top of the backswing. Try it: Take a full backswing and hold it at the top, and then try to lift the left leg. Try the opposite: Make a full downswing and hold it at the finish and lift the right leg. One should be in good balance in either position and be able to lift either leg depending upon the action. The player goes straight back with the clubhead and then lifts it for the so-called high arc. He does this with the left arm and at the top of the swing he pulls down with it. Ninety per cent of all golfers do not use the right side in making the swing, nor do they use their right arm in making the backswing or the downswing. The power side of golf is left out entirely. Since they are on their left side they cannot drive down and through the ball with the right side.

Anything less than the balance of weight shifted is not a weight shift. Shifting 30 per cent is insufficient. The pivot is humbug. Joe uses a pivot, but not with the legs. You won't see Joe Norwood disciples making a pivot with their legs. They are taught to say "Thank you" when it is called to their attention by "outsiders." Joe simplifies all of the moves and makes them easy to learn, and they are certainly eye-openers to the uninitiated. The uninitiated are apt to say, "Hey, you have a nice-looking swing, but you aren't pivoting." Little do they realize that keeping the legs quiet and not twisting the torso is a result of a great amount of self-discipline.

There are three basic elements: legs, body, and arms. Learn to separate them. The body is the culprit as it robs the arms and shoulders of their power. The rubbery action of the legs combined with a twisting torso will produce the kind of shots that a wounded water buffalo would make.

You will begin to enjoy golf when you acquire the use of powerful arms and shoulders instead of a twisting torso. Lead the heel of the clubhead on the downswing, as the toe of the clubhead cannot be under control without being led by the heel—just another way of staying behind the ball and delaying the hands and swinging inside-out.

A common fault in golf, the right hand and
wrist separating from the right arm, allowing
both arms to stop; the club flips, which loses
control and direction.

The longer the club, the more one feels needed, and instead of pure swing, effort is put into the shot—which only retards the swing. This is where the usual facial grimaces, heaving with the body and shoulders, and putting the stomach into the shot take place. Swing *all* clubs alike using the same amount of effort and rhythm.

Most youngsters are willowy, and they swing the clubhead as if it were a weight on a string. There is great speed in their swing; it isn't retarded by body weight as it is with more mature people who attempt to muscle the clubhead with their body instead of swinging with the arms. The deep secret of the swing is in having a twelve-ounce club swing you instead of you over-powering a twelve-ounce club. A ten-year-old outdrives his mother, and Dad gets a hernia trying to blast one past the brat. Junior's swing takes his body through the shot, whereas Mom and Dad go around the ball in forcing the shot with their bodies.

The body supports tension instead of reducing it. Body action disturbs rhythm. Swinging muscles have rhythm, but lifting muscles do not. The hand-to-arm-to-shoulder move has rhythm in its action. Anyone who has an elbow in operable condition has rhythm. All it has to do is flex, open and close, open and close—and these are all it can do. It must be used, or it is back to the Dark Ages of golf, or "What did I do wrong?"

Joe's swing can be learned in a clothes closet and without the use of clubs —just this book and a willingness to learn. Five minutes a day on the golf-o-metrics will strengthen muscles that have been unused and need to be disciplined. It will teach you the parts of the swing movement and how to use them. Most of the parts are "held," and "how to" is clearly outlined. You will be able to perform the parts with your eyes closed, and when you own the parts be able to hit a ball straight with the eyes still closed. The No. 1 reason for the golf-o-metrics is to strengthen the player as well as the parts. The player needs to be in condition to stand without effort in the address position and to be able to swing the club lightly. The club must be handled lightly in order to be a swinger. All clubs must be handled lightly. Long clubs, short clubs, light clubs, heavy clubs—these are all handled lightly. Thumb and forefinger control is the secret in handling clubs lightly.

There is no feeling of hitting the ball in a good swing. It is effortless, rhythmic, and light as a feather in feeling. Stop looking for clubhead feel; just swing lightly. Most golfers are intent on moving the shaft and looking for clubhead feel and forever testing new clubs for that magical feeling. The shaft does not move in a good golf swing. Moving the shaft produces erratic results. Elimination of extraneous movement is the goal of Joe's teachings.

Unless the parts of the swing are known, it is futile to watch the pros. They simply are too smooth to be able to detect what is happening during the swing. When the parts of the swing are known, errors or departures from good form are easily spotted, and the end result can be predicted when a departure is made. It is a case of cause and effect.

The essential point in learning the Joe Norwood golf swing is to be able to hold the parts and to discipline oneself to make the moves. The ball is a

Right thumb and finger control. Wrist and arm in Position One, right elbow close to the side.

The right thumb, forefinger, wrist, and elbow
are holding, allowing the right elbow to
straighten by pushing outward and downward
in the direction of the right knee and foot
toward the line of flight.

visual magnet, and the desire to go to the ball is ingrained. The longer one has played, the harder it is to trust the moves and to disregard trying to hit the ball. There simply isn't any substitute for the discipline necessary to acquire the holding power of the individual parts of the swing. In the order of teaching it should be the backswing, the downswing, and legs. The simple basics of good golf are unknown to many accomplished amateurs and professionals. To quote Dwight Nevil, who is a PGA touring pro, "Lots of good golf is played on the pro circuit, but very little real golf knowledge is known." This is the statement he made to Joe Norwood as Nevil saw the immediate results of Joe's application of his knowledge to Nevil's swing.

Admittedly, any type of golf swing can be grooved and scored with, but that is hardly consistent or accurate golf. Body contortions, facial grimaces and "oh no" are all there. Control is very limited. A poor swing is limited, and a good swing is unlimited in its moves and actions.

Almost all golfers compensate, and hardly anyone can hit a ball straight on purpose; therefore the need to develop a compensating swing. Most golfers are pullers and not swingers. Pulling is a natural gift and easy to do—too easy, which makes acquiring a good golf swing very hard indeed. So is rotating, spinning out, and much else. The parts to resist this action have not been strengthened. The fact that many pros display poor form along these lines doesn't make it right.

Pros have more holding power, and they get more swing than pull. The high handicapper has more pull than swing, and he zeros out with an out-side-in swing. All good swings have similarities. Heinz 57 Varieties typifies the answer to the question of what takes place on the downswing. "I wish I knew" is the most honest answer and the one most often heard when the question is asked.

The pro can flail, lift, carry, and commit any type of error on the back-swing, but he comes down inside-out, and almost all is forgiven most of the time. The high handicapper comes up empty because he swings outside-in in his anxiety to go to the ball. Right and wrong are only a hair apart at this point. The difference between right and wrong is the difference between hor-izontal and vertical; the difference between what is generally accepted and the way Joe Norwood teaches.

The player must learn to use the swinging element, learn to take the stom-ach out of the shot as effort overcomes rhythm and robs the shot of its power.

Joe Norwood has positive control at all times, and this is the object of his teachings.

There is much contradiction in all that is said and written about the golf swing. It emphasizes the lack of any recognized authority. Simple basics are evidently unknown, and bad form seems to be condoned. Getting the ball into the hole no matter what is the name of the game, unfortunately.

Golf articles today reflect a sophistication that borders on double talk in trying to describe subjective feelings. The hand-me-downs of over a hundred years ago that were never interpreted properly and misinterpreted since are still being worked on. The experts do not agree on what takes place during the swing. The whole scene in golf teaching is gray. Convenient phraseology covering errors in the swing is glibly spouted, but no one provides a positive corrective program.

Just about everyone and every book has covered the pros and cons of the golf swing, and they all have one thing in common: They all tell you what to do, and they all fail to tell you how it is done and what it is done with. Joe Norwood has the outline on "how to and what with."

The golf swing is not ethereal, or only for the physically endowed, or very young and natural athletes. Be encouraged. As in everything else, individual effort in acquiring the feelings that disciplined parts will give will be greatly rewarded. A repeating swing is what Joe has to offer, and the ability to keep the ball in play goes with his swing. There are four basic parts to his swing. A player is enabled to discipline the known parts and is privileged to recover his swing at all times.

One's golf swing is represented by the sum total of the parts disciplined. The road to acquiring the parts of the swing is not easy. There is nothing more rewarding than this accomplishment. There are peaks and valleys in the learning curve. The factor of control must be earned.

Joe Norwood has a blueprint for you. Take advantage of it. You will love it and yourself. Do away with the frustrations that the unknown has had for you. Become enlightened and enjoy the knowledge Joe has for you.

Most golfers are casual athletes and out of condition, with long layoffs between rounds or practice sessions. They expect wonderful results and berate themselves when performances are not up to expectations. Untrained and undisciplined, they are not equipped to be "instant athletes." Time to spend at driving ranges is hard to come by for many. The work done at a range is hard. Usually it is spent in driving balls. Sweat, calluses, blisters, wear and tear, aching backs and muscles. Joe's golf-o-metrics offers an easier way to learn the golf swing or to iron out the rough spots in the swing. The golf-o-metrics can be practiced indoors, in small spaces, and of course outdoors and on small grassy areas. The driver is the menace to man's ego, and the easiest way to master that club is to leave it in the closet. Eighty-five per cent of what goes into the golf swing is in the chip shot. The stance is the greatest difference. Otherwise the setup is the same, and so is the swing. Being shorter, the swing is easier to control. Practice chipping to a green or on the lawn—five to ten or fifteen yards at most. The use of the grip, the left arm, the take-away, and the downswing all require the same mechanics in making the chip shot. The feelings are the same. You will learn the parts and how to control them about eight times faster practicing a chip shot than you will with a long club. The clubhead only goes to the knee-high position in a chip shot and requires very little effort to make the swing. But the "holding power" required is the same as when a driver is used. Instead of suffering from frustration, you will gain a sense of accomplishment as you develop control. You will learn how to set and hold the left wrist and arm and stay behind the ball. The clubhead won't be passing your hands. You will learn to toss the clubhead with ease and develop a fluid elbow. You will acquire the feeling of centrifugal force under conditions that you can control. Last but not least, you will be proud of the straight line you can impart to the ball and watch it run true from the topspin imparted to it by the use of a fluid elbow.

The ability to control the shot and to be able to repeat it willingly and on purpose will be most rewarding. What is the use of chipping balls when you can't get off of the tee? The best golfers bemoan the fact that they don't have a supershort game, because that is where the score really is and what the game is all about. A short straight drive doesn't involve a penalty, but getting up and down in a minimum of strokes is a wonderful ego-builder, and being dangerous and deadly around the green is a nice way to pay caddy fees.

"Help me, but don't change me" is universal with golfers. Without change there is no way for improvement. The need for change is self-evident. Learn the ABC's and build from a good foundation. Learn and use fundamentals that can be supported through the knowledge of anatomy. Admittedly some people are more graceful than others, or have a keener sense of touch, timing, judgment, co-ordination, etc. Those less gifted have the same privilege of learning the mechanics of the swing and certainly gain the knowledge of the making of the golf swing. The "instant athlete" must realize that he comes equipped with certain weaknesses and errors. Knowledge of the parts will lead to a repeating swing. Practicing the right moves will reduce error. There is no instant cure and no miracles, yet a feeling can hit real soon and shorten the learning curve considerably.

Program yourself to practice every move in sequence and become a consistent performer. A stick shift gear box is programmed in an exact pattern. One doesn't shift gears in an irregular manner or approach it with a "by guess or by gosh" attitude. This parallel applies to the golf-o-metrics. The disciplined parts will result in exact actions, and there won't be unexpected surprises.

The Grip

"Harry Vardon handled the club with both thumbs and forefingers and tossed it lightly," to quote Joe Norwood.

The thumb and forefinger control is stronger and more powerful and affords more finesse. Good chefs and surgeons handle their knives and scalpels with the thumbs and forefingers. They need control and a deft touch. The golfer is in need of the same delicate touch and control.

The forearms have two sets of muscles: light muscles activated by the use of the thumb and forefinger, and heavier muscles when activated by the use of the last three fingers of the hand, or what is called "the back of the hand." Joe's nomenclature is as follows: "In the front" means that the thumb and forefinger are in control; "in the back of the hand" means that the lower part of the hand is in control. The reason for this is as follows: Two golf balls placed in the right hand in a vertical position with the left hand placed on top of the right forearm will put you in position to make your own test. Squeeze the top ball with the thumb and forefinger and feel the upper, or light muscles flex. Release the grip and place the left hand on the lower part of the forearm and grip with the last three fingers and note the activation taking place. The muscles in the lower part of the forearm are heavier and slower than the lighter muscles in the top of the forearm. Repeat both grips and with each one notice the freeness or tightening up of the elbow. The elbow is free when the light muscles are used. Rhythm is in a flexed and freely moving fluid elbow and can best be that way when the thumb and forefinger grip the club. The control and light touch and feel derived from the thumb and forefinger grip speak for themselves.

The thumb and forefinger will remain in control of the grip when they are placed on the shaft first. Once placed, they must retain the grip, and if eased up, the last three fingers of the hand will take over. There are more muscles in the last three fingers of the hand than there are in the thumb and forefinger. Nine against eight. Once the thumb and forefinger lose the con-

The Address. The left thumb pushes downward against the forefinger. The remaining fingers will fall into place, allowing the left wrist to lock the little finger and the entire left hand with the straight left arm.

trol to the back of the hand it cannot recover the lost control. A new grip must be taken.

When the thumb is extended down on the shaft it puts the wrist in a high position. Pulling back on the thumb, or shortening it, allows the wrist to set down, giving it more flexibility.

There are three basic parts to the grip: the pad, which is the first joint of the index finger and the strongest part of the grip; the second joint of the index finger, which is called the hook; and the thumb.

In taking the grip as described here the same holds true for both hands. Exceptions will be noted and detailed.

The palm should be facing down when taking the grip with the left hand. Place the pad of the first joint of the index finger against the shaft and press down. Next, contract the second joint around the shaft like a hook. Place the upper part of the thumb against the shaft and pull it back slightly. This shortens the thumb and creates a wedgelike pressure. This procedure is followed by the right hand when taking the grip also. The placing of the pad on the shaft first gives one the trigger finger that is desired in a good grip. This is the strongest grip that can be taken. The wedgelike pressure is obtained by tightening the thumb against the knuckle joint of the hand and not down toward the tip of the index finger.

The first joint of the index finger and the hand should be in a straight line. There should be no crook, or curl, at the knuckle joint adjoining the hand. This straight line must be retained at all times. This position is a fulcrum when coupled with the seal of the wrist and is detailed in the next chapter.

Calluses are caused by curling the fingers. Merely place the fingers on the shaft lightly. The thumb and forefinger grip is rather tight. Don't change the power of the grip at any time. The speed of the swing will vary but not the grip. Use the same grip for long and short shots. When you are set to deliver on the downswing, the pad of the index finger tightens the thumb/forefinger/wrist, and the power of the arm is applied for the downswing. The key to control is in the use of the thumb and forefinger grip. The thumb and forefinger control will tell you where your clubhead is at all times. The face of the clubhead and the pad of the right index finger are paralleled. A sticky elbow causes loss of speed, creates effort instead of rhythm, when the back muscles of the hand are in control. The club cannot be handled lightly when gripped this way.

To repeat: Hold the club with the right hand, and with the palm down, place the left thumb and forefinger on the shaft first as previously instructed, then merely place the last three fingers on the shaft lightly (don't curl them). The pad of the first joint of the index finger is pressed against the shaft, then the hook of the second joint, and then the thumb, pulling it back a bit. Be sure that the top half of the thumb rests against the shaft and that the thumb is tightened toward the first knuckle of the hand. Make sure that the first joint of the index finger and the hand form a straight line. The thumb is not placed on the top of the shaft but on the side, and the pressure from the thumb is toward the knuckle of the hand, creating a viselike pressure from side to side. The thumb does not press downward toward the index finger. Repeat the same procedure with the right hand. (1) Press the pad of the first joint of the index finger against the shaft. (2) Draw the hook around the shaft. (3) Place the top half of the thumb against the shaft and draw it back slightly. (4) Set the seal of the wrist. Now you have packaged the grip and are ready for the swing to take place via the flexed, or open elbow. The inward move of the wrist hoods the clubface slightly, and the dimple should be in the eleven-o'clock position.

To maintain compression, the grip must be retained for two seconds after impact. Too many times the grip is eased up at the point of contact or sooner. Count two seconds after each shot, period. Don't lose compression. Maintain the tight grip and you will retain the compression in the shot. This applies to every shot and each and every club used at any and all times. White knuckles and red fingertips do not mean a stranglehold on the club. They merely are signs of a firm grip.

A wonderful way to apply a golf-o-metric is to squeeze a ball between the thumb and forefinger only. Squeeze and hold, release, repeat, and when you think you are squeezing hard, squeeze some more. In a few weeks strong thumbs and forefingers will be developed. The stronger they become, the lighter you will handle the club and refrain from grabbing and clutching with the last three fingers of the hand. The stronger the proper grip becomes, the more confidence you will have in the light, easy feeling, and the more control you will maintain.

Handling a golf ball is an excellent way to develop the power in the thumb and forefinger. It may be a bit clumsy at first, but you will soon become adept at handling the ball. With a ball held in the left hand, press it against the pad of the right index finger, contract the hook around it, then place the top half of the thumb against the ball and squeeze. Remove the thumb. The dimples should be on the top half of the thumb. Repeat the procedure and squeeze, and when you think you are squeezing hard, squeeze some more. Do this exercise as many times a day as you like and for at least three weeks. Develop the parts now and they will work for you later. You will be able to handle the clubs lightly. Lightly does not mean loosely. Joe wants white knuckles and red fingertips at all times. Just a bit of dynamic tension set up without clutching. Keep the first knuckle of the hand flat. The hand and the first joint form a straight line.

"In the front" is the key to control. This is where and how a driver can be swung with no more effort than it takes to sign your name with a pen. What a beautiful sight to see the ease in which Julius Boros handles his clubs. How free and easy it looks. You can rest assured that he has a dynamic tension setup in every move he makes. It is a matter of using the right muscles; properly trained muscles will do the job with ease. Otherwise the player is doomed to struggle.

The proper grip will show the vee of the left hand pointing to the right shoulder and the vee of the right hand pointing to the left side of the chin.

A long index finger and a short thumb will produce a concave wrist. A short index finger and a long thumb will result in a convex wrist, or a high wrist. For flexibility the wrist must be set down. The first joint of the index finger from the hand is placed on the shaft, the knuckle is down, flattened, not curled, making a straight line.

In order to have a one-piece swing, all parts must be unified. You cannot start out with individual, or independent, parts and transfer to a one-piece swing. The grip in total must be a sealed unit in order to function properly.

The inward press of the right wrist becomes magnified power; it makes a fulcrum of the right hand. This is the strongest grip that can be taken. The inward press must be retained throughout the swing. It is the key to control, and when you acquire control of these parts you too will look beautiful *à la* Julius Boros.

[Illustrations of the grip begin on the following page.]

Right-hand control. Place the ball against the right forefinger. Then hook the forefinger against the straight line of the forefinger.

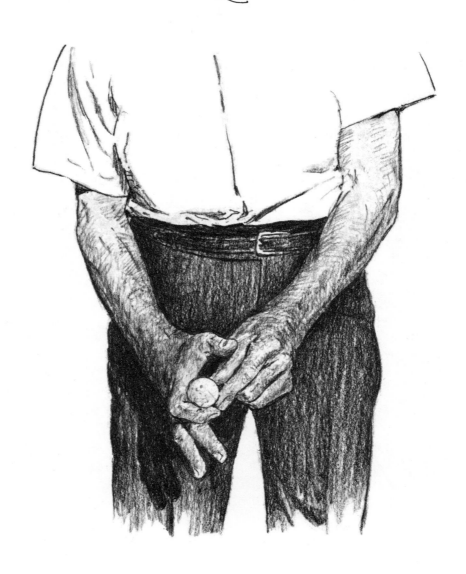

Now place the right thumb by pushing
downward against the ball. Practice for a
perfect V position.

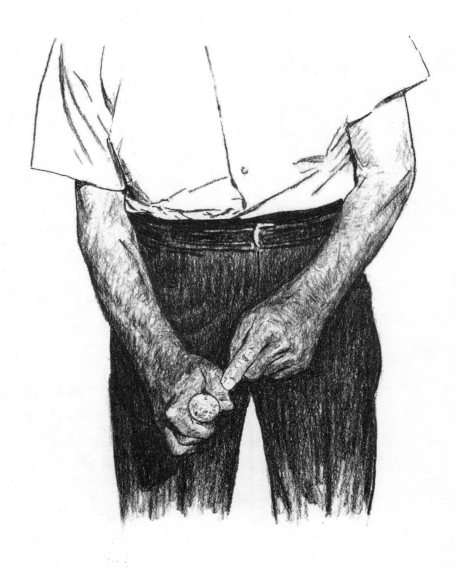

This position shows the perfect "V" in the
direction of the left shoulder.

Now push the right thumb downward to the right forefinger on the club, with the "V" formed in the direction to the left side of your chin. The remaining fingers can be a natural grip, interlock, or overlap, whichever suits your feeling. The hands firm with the right elbow flexed. This allows the right thumb and forefinger to start the backswing in a circular motion.

The Seal of the Wrist

The right hand is an oscillator, and being so it can hardly repeat a move with any consistency. The hand is always willing and anxious to get into the act; it is almost impossible to keep it from doing so. The hand becomes triggered like the release of a slingshot. How does one keep the hand from casting, and what delays the hands in shot-making?

Physically the hand is like a wet noodle compared to the power of the arm. Therefore it is quite obvious that the arm is what should be used to strike at the ball. Extension of the arm cannot be furthered by the hand. *Casting with the hand will not extend the arm, but extending the arm first will delay the hand.* The hand shoots out the second the arm stops its extension. The power of the arm is lost when the hand is cast. Full power of the arm is achieved by making a full extension. Most golfers still have one or two inches of extension left at impact, and are being robbed of added power and distance that is rightfully theirs, as the added extension requires no additional effort. Lack of extension also permits the hands to roll over, causing erratic shots.

The clubhead never passes the hands in any good shot, nor should the shaft move in any shot. Active hands will make the shaft move, and the clubhead will pass the hands, exaggerating any pull already begun by the knees, body, and shoulders. To reduce variations, the shaft must remain still —otherwise the hands will oblige you with a choice among a hook, slice, topped shot, skied shot, and even a whiff. The arm will produce the action that will result in hitting a ball straight. This is covered in another chapter.

The right wrist is set down in a very slight move that is down and inward. This elevates the thumb and forefinger, putting the index-finger knuckle higher than the thumb. The act of setting the wrist down will elevate the toe of the club a fraction, and the inward press of the wrist will hood the clubface. Practice the setting down of the right wrist without a club and be sure you don't lift the thumb and forefinger. The seal of the wrist is made by setting the wrist down. There is a great difference in the way this is done.

Right-hand control. The right thumb presses downward against the forefinger. The right wrist is drawn inward to the eleven-o'clock position. This gives the entire hand a hooded feeling, which raises the index knuckle higher thàn the thumb for starting the backswing circular motion.

Left-hand and -arm control. Entire straight left hand, wrist, and arm, the little knuckle in a downward position for retaining the control and power, locking the wrist and the clubface straight.

By comparison. The left hand and wrist
turned upward, changing the face of the club.
Knuckles up change and reduce the control
with no power for holding.

High wrists are *verboten,* as they are "woody" and lack flexibility and suppleness. Setting the wrists down will give you a smoother feeling throughout the swing. The feeling of the wrists being down must be maintained at all times, in all shots, whether it be a two-hundred-yard drive or a fourteen-inch putt. Sealing the wrist, or setting it down, makes a one-piece unit of the hand and forearm. Any activation of the thumb and forefinger will move the elbow, which in turn activates the arm. The seal of the wrist assures the player that he need not fear the unexpected from a flippy hand. The hand no longer is an oscillating threat every time the club is swung. Remember, the elbow is in a flexed position at all times and begins its journey with the activation of the thumb and forefinger and the inward move of the dimple of the right wrist. It is a package. The first pad below the large knuckle of the right index finger is No. 1; the second joint, or the hook, is No. 2; the thumb is No. 3; the inward press of the wrist dimple is No. 4; and the open, or flexed, elbow is No. 5. When the dimple is set at the eleven-o'clock position, ignition takes place, the swing is on its way. The elbow is open, flexed, or tucked in and always "at the ready position." The elbow will be a blocker if it isn't in the open position, and then it becomes detoured. Blocking the elbow short-circuits centrifugal force. There is no centrifugal force in a straight line, and going back from the ball in a straight line and then into a lift will not create centrifugal force. Traveling on a track that guarantees an arc, which is any part of a circle, will produce centrifugal force. The elbow must be supple at all times and in every shot; it must be in the "ready" position.

The hand, being an oscillator, can move in four directions and make a circle too—five ways for the hand to make trouble for the golfer. A very risky element at best. Couple this high-risk element with a weak left wrist and you can understand why it is so difficult to hit a ball straight on purpose. With these variables golf certainly is an individual effort and not because of the characteristics of the individual physique. Golfers run hot and cold depending upon the feel of the hands on any particular day. The oscillator isn't a very consistent performer. Loss of power and direction are assured when the player uses the hands in shot-making. The hand can go from side to side and up and down and rotate in a circle. Wonderful in itself, but you can't touch your nose or scratch an ear without using the elbow.

The elbow is probably the most dependable part involved in the golf swing. It is impossible to roll an elbow by itself; only with the use of the arm is it possible to roll an elbow. The elbow will operate with the consistency of a punch press or a door hinge. It will repeat itself over and over, producing an exact move each and every time. The only variable in the elbow is the speed factor, and this is supplied by the user of same. Judgment is the only variable. Mechanically the elbow operates the same for everyone. All the elbow can do is open and close, and what makes golf tough is the fact that very few golfers—and this includes a lot of pros—use the elbow during the swing. The seal of the wrist has removed the oscillating hand and tied it in with a smooth operating mechanism that is completely dependable in its movement. This is the "hidden secret" of a repeating golf swing. The use of the elbow provides the speed necessary to move the golf ball, and brute strength or power is an unnecessary element. A repeating swing will keep the ball in play at all times. Learn to use the elbow and learn to trust the moves it makes and you will become a consistent performer.

How to set the left wrist for the right-handed golfer is outlined in the chapter covering the left arm.

When the seal of the wrist is retained, the pad of the index finger of the right hand and the clubface are one and the same. Thus the feeling of knowing where the clubhead is at all times.

The dimple at the base of the right thumb in a twelve-o'clock position should be looking straight up at the sky and will be in a neutral position. In the one-o'clock position the hand will be laid back or open. In the eleven-o'clock position the blade will be hooded, and this is the strongest position the hand/wrist can be in. The dimples of the wrist and elbow will be in alignment. The inward press cocks the wrist to its maximum position and ignites the backswing.

During the Los Angeles Open of 1934 the best round Horton Smith had was a seventy-four. He had hardly won caddy fees the previous three years. Johnny Dawson, one of the most eminent amateurs of that period, brought Smith to Joe Norwood. Joe watched Horton hit a few balls and gave him the tip about the seal of the wrist and the power of the right arm. Horton remarked that everyone had been telling him that his problem was too much right hand. Joe convinced him that he didn't have *any* right arm in his swing. Horton set the seal and hit about six balls and exclaimed that this was the feeling that he had lost. Horton Smith went on to win the very first Masters Tournament at Augusta that spring.

Johnny Miller started out the 1975 season by winning the Tucson and Phoenix opens for the second straight year. The scene now is the Los Angeles Open at the Riviera Country Club, the day of the Pro-Am on the practice tee. The following was twice repeated to his caddy, and this is a direct quote: "I'm setting my wrist down now, and I have a new swing." Several happy adjectives followed. "What am I going to do about the three-wood? It sets differently now; I won't be able to use it." He was swinging a driver and really busting the balls far and straight. He was overjoyed and bursting with enthusiasm over the new swing and the feeling it had given him. A two-time winner so early in the season, one wouldn't think it possible for a premier player to have just "discovered" a new swing. Joe has known this "great secret" for many years and can teach it in three seconds.

The seal of the wrist must be retained through the swing. Once released, there is no such thing as resetting it during the swing. A new grip must be taken. Don't try to recapture the security of the sealed wrist without doing so, unless you feel you can afford to gamble with the shot. To release the wrist is only a hairline move. A fractional move of a wrinkle and it is released. The movement of a wrinkle on the wrist during the downswing with a putter is an absolute guarantee that the seal of the wrist has been lost and the assurance that a push or a pull will take place during the putting stroke. A wristy shot covers a multitude of phrases, which covers a lot of errors. You lifted your head, you looked up, you didn't pivot, your hands were late, your hands got ahead of the ball, etc.

Walter J. Travis told Joe to keep the wrist set for two to three inches after the ball was stroked with a putter. Stuart Maiden, who was close to Bobby Jones, whom Joe met in Atlanta many years ago, said to Joe, "Bobby said that the feeling was hooded," and there is no doubt that Bobby Jones set the seal of his wrist also.

A ball will only be hit on a straight line by the use of the arm, and any release of the wrist will introduce errors. An open wrist will cause a fade or partial slice as example.

There are only two moving parts to contend with in the use of the right arm during the golf swing: the wrist and the elbow. The hand has no privilege when the wrist seal is retained. The wrist is three times faster than the arm. On the downswing the elbow stops when the wrist opens, and the remaining power, or thrust, is unused. The elbow will go to first base as it should, but the hand will flip over toward third base, and now there is trouble. Hooks and snap hooks.

In setting the seal of the wrist, the forearm muscle feeling is drawn. The feeling is so tight on the backswing, the need to have something to start the downswing causes one to release the seal of the wrist, and the hand becomes a flipper. The action of the arm is left out. Retain the seal of the wrist and use the arm for that powerful thrust at the ball and for controlling the ball on a straight line.

Unless the dimple of the right wrist is held at eleven o'clock, it is not possible to straighten the elbow without great effort when attached to the left arm. It also restricts the follow-through.

One . . . two . . . three . . . ignition. The pad of the first joint of the index finger next to the hand is one . . . the hook of the second joint, two . . . setting the thumb is three. The inward/downward set of the wrist cocks the wrist at its maximum, and ignition takes place. The fluid elbow is ignited, and the track it travels on is short, like the hub of a wheel, and it generates tremendous power and centrifugal force.

Use the same procedure to take the grip and to set the seal of the wrist. Each time a club is gripped it should impress your muscle memory deeper and deeper, providing you adhere to a pattern of discipline. The procedure of taking the grip and setting the seal of the wrist is identical with each and every club. No exceptions! From the driver to the putter the same routine must be followed, and it won't be long before it becomes second nature, feeling very natural and comfortable.

The inward press of the right wrist becomes magnified power, and it makes a fulcrum of the right hand. A fulcrum is stronger than a straight line; this is why the straight line of the left hand is overcome by the right hand so easily. The advocates of weakening the grip of either the left or the right hand will be surprised to learn that it is the lack of retention of the right hand that is the cause of all those hooks and slices. The left wrist must be sealed and retained in its straight-line position, but the right hand in its fulcrum position will prevail unless it is retained.

The left arm ends at the right wrist. The outside line of the left arm will be lost when the seal of the right wrist is taken out of use, or relaxed. The left arm follows the track of the right hand in the takeaway. Should the right hand be laid back, or opened, the left arm will follow on the inside. The importance of the extended arc that can only be accomplished by the left arm traveling in an outside line is detailed in the chapter covering the left arm.

This is a tricky move to acquire. Set the seal and retain it for consistent golf. Enjoy the control of the swing, and you will enjoy the flight of the ball on a straight line even more. Complete confidence in owning your swing any day of the week will enable you to sharpen your sense of timing and judgment, which will reduce errors and result in an overall sound and strong game.

The dimple of the right wrist is your *boss,* make it your boss, as you will not control a straight line in making a putt, nor will you attain pinpoint accuracy with the rest of the clubs. Set the dimple of the wrist in the eleven-o'clock position and retain it during the swing.

[Illustrations begin on the following page.]

Grip control. Placing both hands on the club handle, showing long index fingers and short thumbs. This forces the fingers to contract upward, allowing the knuckles to remain in a straight-line position, making the wrists seal the hands inward for control.

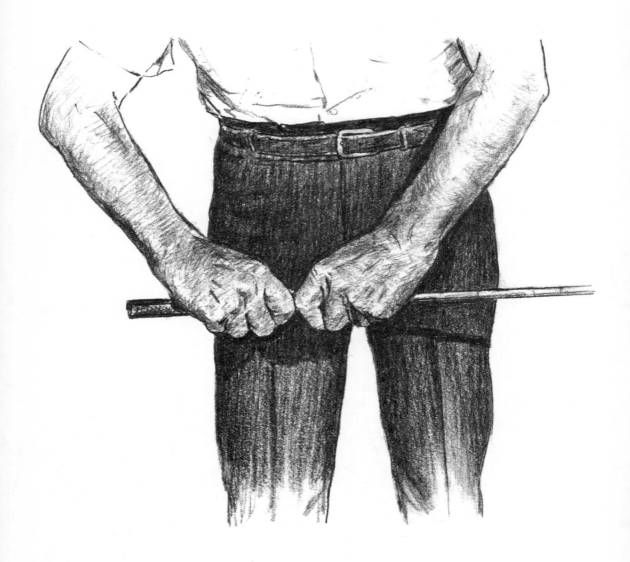

By comparison. Showing long thumbs and short fingers, which removes all hand and wrist power for controlling the club.

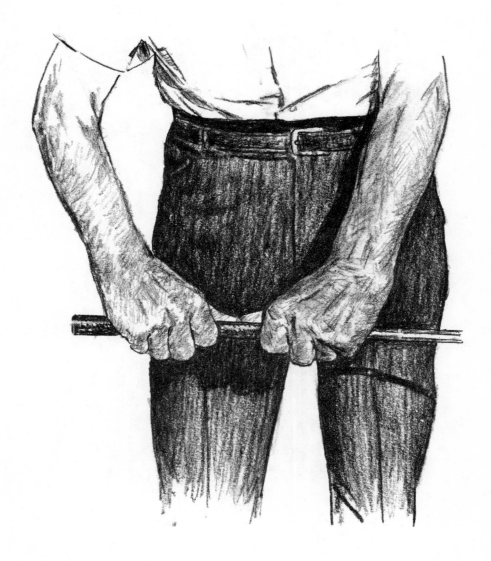

Hand and arm control. Place the left index finger under the index finger of the right hand. Then extend the entire left hand, wrist, and arm. This places the left wrist out in front of your knuckles.

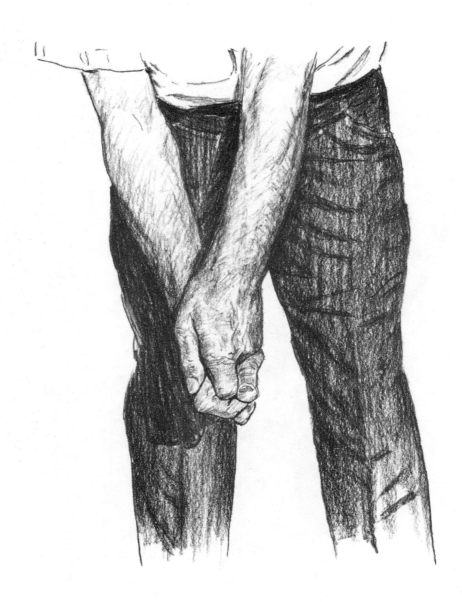

Then pull the right index finger and thumb backward in a circular move with the aid of the right elbow: Position One.

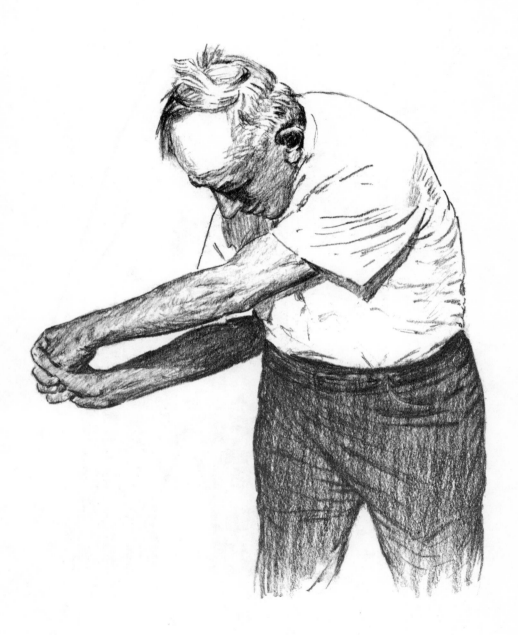

Now push and unfold the right arm in a
vertical downward move, straightening the
entire right arm opposite the right knee, with
both arms extended just before contact.

The Left Arm

The left arm is one of the four major parts of the golf swing. The left arm is the control factor that produces the line that the ball travels on and does so in every shot, from a drive to a putt. The left arm in the Norwood swing is a "holding" unit and not a "pulling" unit.

Most golfers swing the left arm "with the shoulder," using the hand/wrist and elbow to help. Going up or coming down become very uncertain moves with that many parts involved. Very few straight balls can be hit with this type of erratic action. Joe has the golf-o-metric that will develop a sturdy left arm for anyone who will spend one minute a day on the exercise.

Swinging the left arm "with the shoulder" takes the body on an unnecessary trip. Joe swings the left arm *from* the shoulder." Not "with," but "from." The left arm has to be independent of the body. The body is not used in making the swing. The extension out of the shoulder will make this separation. The extensor muscles in the shoulder can extend three to five inches and increase the arc by that many more inches, which in turn creates more centrifugal force.

The left arm has two moving points, which are the wrist and the apex (the inside muscle) of the arm. The elbow can't be rolled and is not considered a moving part. The weakest link in the makeup of the left arm and the golf swing in its entirety is the left wrist. If open at the address position, the wrist will not close or straighten during the swing. The flicking left wrist is the culprit of most bad shots, and it loves to hook.

Golf is a two-handed game. Hold the left and smack it with the right— with the arm, not with the hand.

Load the left with power from the shoulder to the wrist; then the wrist seals the hand, and they become a one-piece unit, from the shoulder to the tip of the club. There are no breaks between the extreme points of the shoulder and clubhead. It is as solid as is the shaft. It becomes a static unit never changing dimension in its length. Retain the holding power in the left arm

Place the arms straight down, with the index fingers together. Now hold the right hand and arm still. Start pushing the left hand, wrist, and arm from the left shoulder—not with the shoulder. A three-inch extension of the left arm will develop the left-arm control for all clubs.

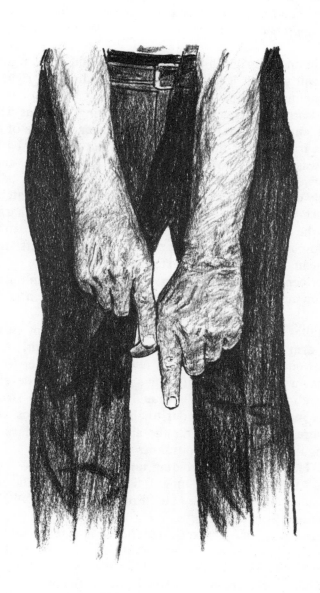

and there won't be any variations in the arc. The hand will not seal the wrist. Set the left hand and then join the arm to it for controlling the line of flight.

Load, unload, and reload. Once release takes place it is impossible to reload in the course of the swing without introducing uncertain results. Whenever the left releases, the right will follow. This sort of makes the right hand more of a villain than it really is in overpowering the left. The left is usually so weak that having the right hand overpower it is certainly no big thing. One must develop the left arm as well as the other parts of the swing. Keep the right hand and arm strong but strengthen the left so it can take a fair amount of pressure. The instant the left releases it ceases to swing and begins to pull.

The left arm and the right hip are teammates, and if the right hip releases, the left arm will go with it also. "How to" regarding the right hip is in the chapter containing the prop.

A weak left arm will come up on the downswing, whereas when it is held, the right will lengthen it, staying on the ball longer. Beware of detours; relax the left arm a fraction and the shoulder is left out. It won't be used, and the charge that was loaded into it will be gone. The eye can hardly spot the difference between a fully charged left arm and one that has been discharged ever so slightly unless one is aware of the specific muscle to watch.

You can't stay behind the ball when the left arm is discharged, as it will pull around the ball. The extensors out of the shoulder can't come down when the elbow is bent. Also, one can't rotate when the left arm is extended but certainly can and will when the extensors are released.

Seventy per cent, or more, of golfers release the left arm during the swing, and this is how and where compression is lost. The crunch is left out at impact.

A few minutes of each practice session should be spent swinging at balls with the left arm only. Swinging from the apex of the arm. A tiny swing is sufficient. Just enough to chip a ball a few yards. This exercise can best and easily be done on the putting green using a putter. This will develop control.

When extending the left arm it should be extended as straight down as possible. The more one reaches out to the ball, or extends away from the body, the more heave or lift with the shoulders takes place. It takes less effort to swing in a more upright position.

To recap: The left arm is a holding unit for the right to hit against. The left arm is set into a one-piece unit. It is swung "from the shoulder," not "with the shoulder" in an outside line. "From" instead of "with" is where the men are separated from the boys.

The left hand is set like a boxer's fist, then it is extended out of the shoulder by using the extensor muscles. Next, tighten the pinky finger; this knocks down the large wrist bone, making the wrist convex. A single unit from the shoulder to the clubhead is now loaded with compression.

Place the butt end of the shaft underneath your left armpit and hold the shaft with the hand and swing it. The arm attached to the shaft acts as a one-piece unit. This is the feeling one should have when the left arm is loaded and retained during the swing. This is the one-piece feeling of arm and club that will produce a straight line each and every time. Most golfers feel that the club is an extension of the wrist instead of the arm. Flicking away at a ball with a puny wrist is no match for a sturdy arm loaded with compression.

An angle is stronger than a straight line. The left hand and forearm is a straight line when the wrist joins the hand. The cocked right hand is an angle. The right hand is the dynamic force and it easily overpowers the left wrist, unless the left wrist is set and held. If nothing else is done to improve the swing, just setting and holding the left wrist will automatically improve the swing of the majority of golfers, imparting a straight line to the ball's flight and a tremendous increase in control.

A convex wrist puts the club behind the hands. Flexing the wrist, or making it concave on the backswing, puts the club in front of the hands. The club should be behind and held with a convex wrist, allowing you to stay behind the ball instead of going around it.

Joe can make swing after swing, and after each swing he can return the clubhead to the original address position, and the blade will be in the same position as before the swing. There is no release of any part during his swing. The left wrist holds its original position at all times in every shot from a drive to a putt. Any release will allow the clubhead to flip-flop. The shaft doesn't move when Joe swings the club. Active hands and wrists will move the shaft, and the chances of meeting the ball with a squared blade are very slim. The ball will fly, and only as directed by the blade. Change the blade and you change the flight of the ball. Don't weaken the right-hand grip to keep from overpowering the left hand. Learn to strengthen the left wrist and retain tight hands on the club. Make a full swing, and after the follow-through, without changing the position of the wrists, return to the address position. Check the position of the blade; compare it to its original position. Try a few swings for consistency.

The reward of a loaded left arm is pinpoint accuracy. Extend and hold. "What an order that is," says Joe. Holding power is not the same as brute strength. An Olympic wrestling champ, with nineteen-inch biceps, couldn't hold a twelve-ounce club in the extended position for ten seconds without quivering. A veteran of twenty years on tour as a pro couldn't either. Girls with a slight build have developed great holding power in a very short time through a golf-o-metrics exercise. The test: take a backswing, and when the arms are about waist high, stop and hold the position. Extend the left arm as much as possible, and remove the right hand from the shaft. Watch for the arm to drop. Continue to hold for a count of ten. After about four or five seconds, providing a full extension has been made, the arm will begin to quiver. Almost anyone, with a bent arm, can hold a club aloft for quite a long time.

A fully loaded left requires the extensor muscles from the shoulder to be extended and will put the arm into the wrist, tightening the pinky finger,

At address, concave vs. convex. The left arm
in a straight-line position, with the left wrist in
a concave position. This produces a
controlling feeling at the address for swinging
the club.

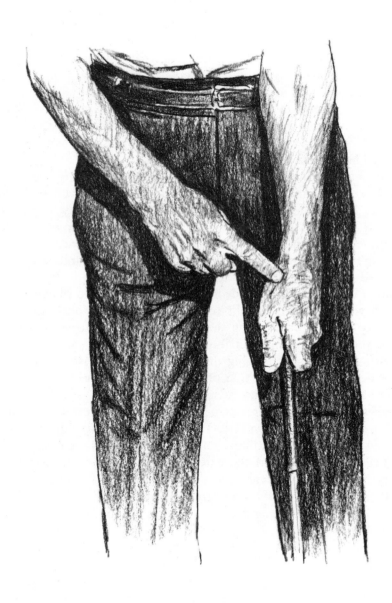

By comparison, the left arm in a straight-line position, with the left wrist in a convex position, giving no feeling of control during the start of the backswing.

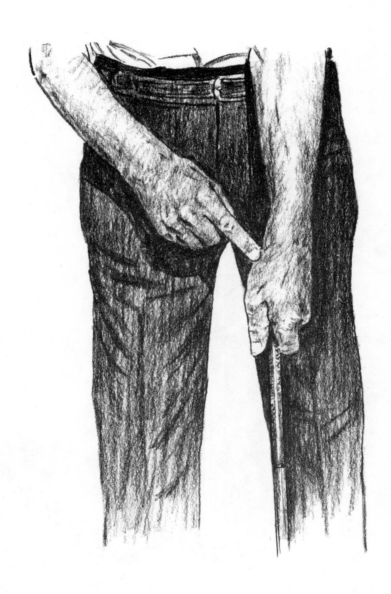

Left-arm control. Position One, the left arm extended and loaded. The right thumb, forefinger, wrist, and elbow have placed the club in a nine-foot swing position. The strongest position known to golf, with no feeling of the use of the left side. The lower part of the body remains in a propped position.

Test the extended left arm by now removing
the right hand to see if the original position is
held. This control is a must for all golfers.

What happens when the right hand is removed. The left arm at the elbow falls inward, pulling away from the right arm, reducing the holding power that starts a rotating movement, and anything can happen.

causing the hand to curl and form a convex wrist, leaving the forearm and wrist in a straight line. Make a fist with extended thumb; this will set a high wrist. Look at the angle this move produces. Note the lack of flexibility in this wrist position. The final requirement, or checkpoint, is to really put some extension into the arm and remove the dimple from the crook of the arm. The feeling here should be taut and the curl in the hand should be tight; when these conditions are met you will find your arm quivering after a few seconds of extension. The loaded left arm should resemble Ben Hogan's left arm. Find a picture in an old magazine and use it as a model.

The wrist positions the blade, which in turn controls the flight and direction of the ball. A change in the wrist position will make a corresponding change in the face of the blade. The wrist must not be broken inwardly or outwardly; it is to be set at the address, in its proper position, and retained during the entire swing and follow-through.

Men with biceps the size of a small telephone pole groan and grunt trying to hold a twelve-ounce club, while the left arm is quivering like a bowl of Jell-O in trying to hold a fully extended left arm. People of the opposite build in physique are able to acquire the holding power. It is a matter of knowing what to put into the act and not brute strength. Follow a routine to develop the left arm, and it will work for you. The quiver that sets into the left is further proof of a weak left arm. Very few untrained golfers can hold an extended left arm for ten seconds without the shakes setting in after four or five seconds. A minute a day with a simple exercise will in a short time develop a considerable amount of holding power. An extension of one to two inches and the power to hold it during the swing will transform an average golfer from hacker to pro status in appearance.

Pros are quoted as saying that Ben Hogan, in his playing days, did something they don't do. Hogan probably had the greatest left arm in golf. Joe believes that Hogan could extend five to seven inches. Hogan's accuracy is legendary, and of course proves that he could hold such a tremendous extension. This is what set Hogan apart from the field and what has the pros guessing as to what Ben Hogan did that they don't do. Hogan must have put two to three years into developing that much extension and holding power. Without an effort to put a few weeks into developing a left arm, there is no way to encourage the average golfer. The great arc from that much extension created tremendous centrifugal force for Hogan and is what permitted him to be so long and so straight. Pictures of Hogan showing his extended left arm reveal the flat wrist and the curl in the hand, the pinky finger under a convex wrist. Beautiful!

The extensor muscles come down the arm from the shoulder, and the contracting muscles come up from the hands. Put the pressure into the wrist, from the shoulder which makes a seal, and have a one-piece left arm, which will swing from the apex of the arm effortlessly. One piece from the shoulder to the knuckle of the pinky finger. The left arm will swing from the apex in an outside line. Without the one-piece left arm, the arc is greatly diminished, as the swinging left arm will carry inside.

Facial distortions are the result of stomach muscle action and what Joe means when he says, "Take the stomach out of the shot." When he sees anyone grimacing, he knows effort is being applied by the stomach muscles. A contorted face means that someone is trying to heave a piano about twenty yards instead of swinging the club lightly and effortlessly. Strengthen the left arm and develop the needed holding power by the use of the exercises outlined. Remember, the arm is extended, and extension must be retained. Any release of the extension will change the dimension of the arc and alter the original address position. "Load and hold"; Joe knows the truth of the statement and its importance in the golf swing.

The left hand is contraction support. The arm supporting the hand is extensor support, which as the club gets longer requires more support, and invariably this is where the stomach gets into the shot as it feels that more effort is needed. The extra distance is built into the club and should be swung as easily as a shorter club.

Here is the simple golf-o-metrics exercise that makes use of the extensor muscle that will load the left arm and develop holding power.

Stand up straight, facing a wall, reach out, and touch it with the index finger of the left hand. Step back about three inches and repeat the extension. Do not lean forward with the shoulder or the body. Just reach out from a steady position toward the wall. Repeat this a few times until you are sure that you are stretching the arm toward the wall and not leaning into it. You should be feeling the extensor muscles working by this time.

Next, make a boxer's fist with the left hand and extend it downward out of the shoulder. The extensor should be working in the same manner as it did when trying to reach out to touch the wall. Repeat this downward move several times, being sure to extend from the shoulder. Now that you have a slight feeling of the extensor muscles working for you make a full extension, tighten the pinky finger as it puts a curl into the hand and creates a convex wrist. Do not break the wrist inward when tightening it. The top of the wrist and arm should be in a straight line. The pressure applied to the wrist is downward and not inward.

Stand at ease, and with the left arm in a natural and relaxed position, take it across your body, as in a backswing. Note the heavy dragging feeling in this action. Now extend the left arm downward and take it across the body as before. Note the much lighter feeling in the movement of the arm. Repeat the two moves in order to get acquainted with the different feelings. Repeat the exercise with the arm relaxed and again with the arm loaded. Extended properly, you should have the feeling that the arm traveled by itself. It should move easily and lightly. Try for more extension and repeat the exercise again. Look for the feeling just described.

Now that you know how to do this golf-o-metric, you should program yourself to doing ten of these daily. Make the boxer's fist and extend downward, feeling the extensors out of the shoulder, and take the arm across your body as in making a swing. Hold it in this position for ten seconds. You can do as many sets of this exercise as you like. In about three weeks you will begin to develop a great amount of holding power.

To expand the exercise, reverse the club, grip the shaft about six inches below the clubhead. Repeat the exercise about ten times daily for one full week. The second week slip your hand down the shaft until it is about midway, and repeat the exercise. The third week, take the grip at the end of the shaft and again repeat the exercise during that week. At the end of the third week you should be able to hold the club with the butt end of the shaft fully extended for ten seconds without a quiver, and even smile, proving that the stomach muscles aren't involved. Roll up your sleeve, bare the arm, swing the club waist-high with both hands, remove the right hand, and push the *arm* out, removing the dimple from the elbow. The arm must be taut, fully extended. Check for the curl in the hand. Is the pinky finger tightened? It is fairly easy to leave out the extra effort it takes to remove the dimple in the elbow. It is even easier to relax the curl in the hand instead of maintaining the stretch. These are the checkpoints. Do it right and you will begin to enjoy golf.

As you become more adept at doing this exercise and as it becomes easier to do, check the checkpoints. You must put forth full effort at all times. You must develop the holding power and compression to become a good golfer. You will hit the ball with authority, and the sound at impact will be entirely different. The compression at impact will amaze you. You will know it and feel it. You will begin to look like a class golfer with that left arm extended in a professional manner. There is nothing better looking than an extended left arm during a golf swing. Without this holding power it isn't possible to handle a club lightly and to swing without effort. There must not be any slack from the shoulder down to the clubhead.

Take the grip with the thumb and forefinger, get the pinky finger tightened by setting the wrist to lock the hand while the arm is being extended, and swing from the apex. The left arm should form a straight line from the shoulder to the clubhead. There should not be a detour at the left wrist. The wrist is set down and not high, with two knuckles showing.

The left wrist and left knee produce the majority of errors in making the golf swing. You can include topped shots, fat shots, hooks, and slices too. Develop a holding left arm and simplify the swing by reducing the privilege of making errors.

In the address position the left arm will be in front of the left thigh at all times for every shot. Generally speaking, you will find that the most suitable spot to play the ball from is off the left heel for all shots.

First place the body in an upright position, as illustrated. Then with the use of a short iron, you place the left hand at the head of the club as illustrated. Now extend the entire left arm downward from your left shoulder. The straight line from the shoulder to the hand shows the left wrist in a convex position, with the knuckles turned down. Now place the right hand on the handle, with the right wrist in a concave cocked position turned upward. The right elbow is folding in a vertical position. Due to the angle, this produces the most powerful position known in golf.

The body position remains the same. The straight left-hand wrist and arm show no change. The right hand and concave wrist remain in a cocked position as the right arm pushes downward from out of the right shoulder in a vertical direction. This pushing motion with different speeds downward with the straight right arm will eliminate any pulling by the left arm. This is one golf-o-metric you can't pass up.

The Prop

The base of the swing is in your feet. A gyroscope should rest on a solid foundation so that its functions are not disturbed. The torso should also rest on a solid base, one that is strong enough to give adequate support to the movements thrust upon it. Both legs must hold and work as a team, each doing its part. They should give such solid support that there is complete freedom of movement for the arms and shoulders.

The prop is concerned with what happens below the waist—no more and no less. Hips, thighs, legs, ankles, and feet—all of these parts have a place in the swing. Some are active, and others are holding parts. Disciplining the holding parts to hold is the hard part.

It stands to reason that taking aim at a tiny target would require stability. The good golf swing requires a quiet body and active arms. Body movement is the ruination of the golf swing.

Not to belabor the "instant athlete," but try this test to satisfy yourself. Stand with both feet together and then lift one foot off the ground. Stand for ten seconds, if you can, and shortly you will feel the quiver in the ankle and see it wobble around. Try it with the other foot and note the identical result. Throwing the mass of the body onto legs and ankles that aren't strong enough to support the action leads to very erratic results. Spend ten seconds a day balancing on each leg, and at the end of three months you will have overcome the quiver in what you previously thought were very strong legs and ankles. The legs will take the least lines of resistance when the body weight is thrust upon them. Being in less than superb condition when called upon to accept the overload, they will take the easy way out and fail to support the action. The easy way is not always the correct way and in this case will usually lead to disaster.

The basics must be practiced, and sufficient time to acquire them should be allowed for in the program being outlined. This may be discouraging to some, but for the serious golfer who wants to progress, this will be encouraging, as the future benefits are great. Acquiring a repeating swing is the primary goal.

The customary stance is composed of a forward press, then back onto the right leg with the backswing, then forward again with the downswing, and one hopes that all parts will be timed well and get there together at the point of impact. Why not eliminate two uncertain moves and start out in a "ready position" that will get you to the ball in an exact movement? There is no customary pivot in the Joe Norwood style. Instead of a forward press, why not a backward press and eliminate two moves? Simplify the swing and all that goes into it. The average golfer hikes up on the backswing, putting the hip into a high position. Why not start out that way? Minimize an uncertain move in doing so. Replace the uncertain move with a positive one. Place the left leg and knee in a position that will reinforce the right leg. This reinforces the right thigh like a crossbrace, and everyone knows how strong a crossbrace always is in supporting whatever it is used for.

The golfer must be trained to "stay in his shoes" during the swing. He must stay down in the address position during the backswing, and on the downswing he must go below the address position. The only way the golfer moves his head, or comes off the ball as a rule, is by coming up "out of his shoes." Keeping the feet quiet will keep the head still and eliminate a good deal of rigidity at the address position.

Joe sets up on a "prop" that is in a "ready to go" position. He has eliminated the two uncertain moves. He is dynamically poised and ready for action, just as any alert athlete would be in returning a tennis ball, throwing a punch, doing a broad jump, or executing a pivoting move in basketball. People in action are all alert and poised for action. They aren't back on their heels, nor are they in a relaxed condition. There is dynamic tension present, and this does not mean rigidity or nervous tension, which tightens muscles.

An open stance should be used whenever the bulk of the weight is on the left side. All the short shots should be made with the weight predominantly on the left side. All putts, and all pitch and chip shots fall into this category. A short shot with the weight on the left side can range up to ninety or one hundred yards. Sixty-five per cent of the weight should be on the left side at the very least.

The closed stance allows the arms to arrive in Position One easier, as the distance traveled is shorter. The open stance has no power, the body rotates, and takes longer to get to; the closed stances takes the power unleashed on the downswing instantly. You have seen many pictures of pros rolling out on the left foot, but this doesn't make it right, as it is very poor form, a sign of weakness and lack of knowledge. The downswing should go into the hips, whereas the pull in the downswing goes into the ankles, causing one to roll out on the left foot. These pros should be hitting to a left side that is strong enough to accommodate the weight shift, but the rollout takes place because of the weakness in the supporting unit. Some pros even teach an exaggerated turn with the hips and do a leg rollout that is extreme. Everyone comes equipped with this weakness, so why teach it? A great many pros don't know how to stand and have no knowledge of the basics involved in the stance. Those unexpected hooks wouldn't occur if they knew what the left leg, knee, and foot had to do to support them in this crucial action. The source of "What did I do wrong?" is oftentimes soft leg muscles for the high handicapper.

The player should be in good balance at all times. Go to the top of the backswing and hold it there, then lift the left foot off the ground. If you are unable to do so without a further shift in weight, you are without a doubt still on your left side. You have not made a transfer of weight to the right side and will be unable to go to the left side on the downswing. Now to test the opposite side of the swing and stance. Make a complete swing, a full backswing, and a full downswing, and hold the finish. Lift your right leg up off the ground while in that position. Again, you should be in good balance on your left leg. If you are not, obviously a weight shift did not take place on the downswing.

Substitute the forward press with the backward press. Eliminate the two uncertain moves that require such perfect timing. Eliminate the extra wavelengths introduced by those extra moves. The pull and devastating action resulting from the rotation caused by the pull will also be eliminated. The counterpart of the left wrist is the left knee. The left knee is the weakest link and should be the strongest, as it has to take the brunt of the downswing with the body added to it. The body is added to the swing, it does not go before the swing. The labor in making the backswing is reduced when the left knee is held in its proper position, which is inward.

The fourth major part is the left knee. Putting the left knee in its proper position and retaining it would be like bracing a vertical member with an angle, strengthening it much as a carpenter braces a stud. The left knee braces the right thigh and forces the right hip higher. In the backswing there is no movement in the right leg when properly braced and held. One could say there is no movement in the legs during the backswing. Actually, the only movement that takes place is in the left knee, and that is a very small move.

You will seldom see a rear pocket on a good pro rotating on the backswing, as they all brace themselves in some manner. However, the misconception of getting the hips out of the way causes them to roll out, with the left knee and foot on the downswing. Many of them are very strong, as they should be, but collapse at impact, showing very poor form in the follow-through stage of the swing. Stay on the right side with the left knee quiet and "go to the left leg"—not with it. Reduce variations by having a quiet body. Some of the pros would be unbeatable were they aware of the ABC's of proper footwork. They certainly would be more consistent and straighter and not in constant fear of the unexpected. The fear of the unknown keeps them in an "uptight" condition.

The legs and body shouldn't be locked up as a single unit. The legs should be in a strong position to support the torso. This gives the shoulders the lib-

The right leg in a straight-line position from the knee to the foot. A backward press with the left knee places the right hip in a propped position. There is 70 per cent weight on the right side, with 30 per cent weight on the left side at the address. This sitting position reduces body motion during the backswing.

erty to move as independent units. Too wide a stance tightens the thigh muscles and sets up too much energy. Rotating the shoulders puts a twist into the ankles. When the shoulders work in the pulleylike fashion, or north and south, it puts the action into the hip. This is where the action should be at all times. The thighs set the knees, legs, and feet. When the left leg goes first, as in a rotation, the right will follow it. The left leg holds and the action is set off, or triggered, by the right leg, which transfers the power of the right side to a strong left side. You "go to the left and not with it," retain the power of the left, or dissipate it by rotating.

The golf-o-metrics involved in assuming the prop are detailed as follows: Stand erect with both feet together, ankle bones touching, with no movement of the body. Place the left foot away and ahead about three inches, with the toe pointing out at a forty-five-degree angle. This will lower the right buttock and give a feeling of sitting on the right hip. The right foot is straight, as it should be for all shots. The right foot should parallel the face of the blade at all times, except when the clubhead is laid back for a cut shot, or whatever. Unless the right foot is straight, the right knee will not go down into the right foot. A turned-out toe will nullify this move. The right knee is studded and held in this position during the entire backswing. It does not move one iota; it should be as sturdy as a fence post in order to support the action to be thrust upon it. Most golfers will let the right knee back up from one to three inches. This permits swaying, rotating, back pockets turning with swiveling hips. These are all signs of a very weak and incorrect setup.

After the placement of the left foot out at the forty-five-degree angle and the foregoing have taken place, tuck the left knee inward behind the ball. This is done by relaxing the left kneecap and letting it drop down and in. Now comes the hard part. The left knee, to be effective, must be held in this position during the entire backswing. When this is done properly the feeling of having the left knee bracing the right leg and forcing the right hip up should have been felt. When held, this allows the shoulders to operate easier and will reduce the amount of effort necessary to make a smooth backswing.

The golfer's right side is supposed to be driving downward in the downswing against a holding left side; instead, courtesy of the rotating hips and knees, he crosses the line of flight and rolls out on the left foot, even comes up on it. Pictures show pros back on the left heel and with the left toe in the air an inch or two, some even curled up, or rolled outward on the left foot. The inconsistency is obvious. The right side is supposed to drive to the left leg and not with it, and both sides must go below the address position. One side driving down with the other coming up promotes all sorts of errors.

Lighten the torso when taking the prop also. Inhale and retain the breath during the swing. This will lessen the weight of the upper body by about ten pounds, and it then won't require as much labor to make the heave-ho in the event that you make your "natural" swing. Should you make Joe's swing, it will take even less effort than normally required. Program yourself to lighten your torso with every shot, putts included. Holding your breath will give you an added benefit. It will enable you to draw a steady bead on your target, just as a rifleman does. Draw and hold the aim. It takes only a few seconds for the action to take place.

Always, in assuming the address position, whether it be on the right side or the left, have the toes gripping inside of your shoes—gripping, just as if you were barefoot. Added to the other elements of the proper stance, this will give you a solid and immovable stance—strong as the Rock of Gibraltar.

The Crosslateral Move

"Ben Hogan never left his big toe," says Joe. It has been written that Ben Hogan had the feeling of pushing off the big toe of the right foot. All due respect to the articles written about this feeling, or action, but pushing off the big toe is actually the last thing that happens in the downswing.

Most advocate initiating the downswing by pulling the hips out of the way, or going with the right knee first. Many people have diversified feelings of what actually takes place, and when, as regards this bit of action.

"How to and what to do it with"—let's follow a bit of Joe Norwood's technique.

Basically there are three ways to get the hips out of the way: rotation, the straight lateral, or the Joe Norwood crosslateral. The first is self-explanatory; the second is a lateral shift, or slide, then a rotation. All but the crosslateral are very uncertain moves at best. The first two moves will take you over the little toe of the left foot. Rolling out diminishes the power of the left side. The left side is a holding unit so that the right side can hit against it; it can't be if it is spinning away from the right side.

The crosslateral move takes you to the big toe of the left foot. The knee travels on the inside of the instep on its way to the big toe of the left foot. It doesn't roll out, crossing over the instep of the foot. This is an exact move, and can be repeated over and over with predetermined results, instead of the varying movement of a rotation.

"Iron Mike" is what Joe calls his right leg. Not only does it support the major share of the weight distribution, but it also must take the shock of the downswing.

The player has assumed the proper stance on his prop at the address position and has made his backswing and all is in readiness for the start of the downswing. The right hip, not the right knee, initiates the crosslateral by driving down. "The right hip is the sweetheart of motion," says Joe. The hip moves the upper and lower parts of the body. The hip moves the thigh, knee, leg, and foot. The right hip is the cause and the left leg is the effect. The right is the "giver" and the left is the "taker." This is true of the left and right arms also. The hip goes into the crosslateral, whereas the rotating action goes into the ankles. On the backswing the right arm cranks up into the shoulder, which forces the left shoulder down, and at this point goes into the right hip in feeling. The shoulders tilt, and here is where the pulley action of the shoulders takes place, and this is Joe's pivot. When the left shoulder goes down it puts more torque into the right thigh and hip.

Introducing the "sitter." This is where and how compression originates. This is what generates compression. This is the first split second of the downswing.

The right hip initiates the move, and it becomes a downward thrust forcing the knee to pound down onto the ball joint of the big toe. For a split second Sam Snead and Lee Trevino look like they are riding a bronco. Action pictures of them reveal this very clearly. This action is a momentary *sitz*. The player literally jumps at the ball. All of the action is thrusting downward. Here is where the right leg performs the heroics that earn it the name of "Iron Mike." It is supporting the downward thrust of arms and shoulders as well as the torso, and of course supporting the body on the backswing also, enabling hands and arms and shoulders to work freely. This is a very short move and of split-second duration.

Ride 'em, cowboy! The hips go into the knees. Don't swivel, pivot, sway, turn, or twist with the legs. The strongest part of the golf swing is in the legs. They are supporting elements and are not to be used in a rotating or twisting action. The legs cannot match the speed of the downswing therefore the player should keep them still, or quiet.

Various golf articles show pictures and captions of where the plane of the shaft drops due to the action of getting the hips out of the way. Believing that the change of the plane is based on this is a false conception. What really happens is that the "sitter" does a *sitz,* and the shaft seems to drop. The golfer is driving downward and goes below the address position. Most golfers come up from the address position. Coming above the address position causes the golfer to lose much of his compression. The position of the knees at the address position is the reference point, and in a proper swing the knees need to go below the starting point.

At the start of the downswing the left knee is held inward and bracing the right leg, pushing the right hip into its high position. When the *sitz* takes place, the left knee moves toward the big toe about three to five inches, staying on the inside of the instep of the left foot. However strong your left knee is, or how active you are with the "sitter" will govern whatever you put forth initially. A weak left knee will not be supportive and will take the line of least resistance by rolling out. Trying to put a thrust onto the left knee requires it to be held inward. You can't make a two-inch thrust and then decide to add to it. You make the maximum move on the first thrust. The maximum move is made for all shots, always, but the pressure and speed will vary depending on the distance of the shot.

Lower part of the body is in a sitting position, measuring about four inches below regular height. Upper part of the body has a slight change due to the left shoulder lowering downward in the direction of the ball during the backswing. On the downward swing, the right arm and right side must lower in a vertical downward motion below the four-inch starting position; otherwise the body will straighten up, reducing power and control.

The left toe must be turned to at least a forty-five-degree angle to allow enough room for the crosslateral to take place. Squared feet will not permit this smooth action.

The crosslateral puts you behind the ball, enabling you to go down and through and not around, as in a rotating knee action. The body is designed to rotate; encouraged by a rotating left knee, it will retard the use of the arms and reduce freedom of action.

Anything that moves from the waist down disturbs the swing. The waist, thighs, legs, and feet are in a balance of themselves.

The magnified power of the coil achieved on the backswing must be retained in order that it may be used at the right time. Going with the right knee first releases this stored power. There is no compression when the right knee goes before the swing. The body weight doesn't get into the shot unless the tension is retained. The experience of pulling, or trying to roll up a window shade after the spring has fizzled is very similar. The right hip is the master unit, and then when it triggers the *sitz* and the legs go into the crosslateral the hit is made, and then, and only then, is the weight of the body added to the swing. Body weight is added to the swing and not used to make the swing by injecting effort and disturbing rhythm. The knees drive downward; it is a magnified driving force and not a dissipating power. The swing takes the body, the body does not take the swing. Stay on the right side as long as possible, and stay there tight. The swing will take you, and then it will be the right time to add the body; it will do so automatically.

"The old Scots used to say, 'Go doon,' but they didn't tell you what to do it with," says Joe. Stay in your shoes, don't come up out of them. Staying down will do away with the body lift, straightening up, topping the ball, lifting your head, etc. Most people will tell you that you lifted your head when actually you didn't stay down in your shoes. Whenever you come above the address position you will introduce errors and variations. Swinging with the hands shortens the arc and can be blamed for tearing up a lot of nice turf. You must go below the address position in every shot that has a down, or a vertical move in it. You seldom see a flat left foot in a golf swing. The right side is driving down and the left foot is coming up, or rolling over. When the left knee travels alongside the instep of the left foot, the left knee exerts great pressure under the left big toe. Joe says, "he cracks walnuts under his left big toe." Pushed or pulled shots are the result of rolling out with the left knee and foot. The crosslateral becomes a structured action and is a repeating track, or swing plane. The elements involved are stable, and the move is short and can be repeated with a minimum of error.

Getting up on the left leg is what delays the hit. The longer you travel onto the knee in the crosslateral the longer the hit is delayed. The shorter the distance the knee travels the sooner the swing goes around the ball. Whatever the knee takes first is the maximum, as you can't further this move once the downswing begins. Maximum follow-through is achieved by getting onto the left knee to its fullest extent.

The weak left ankle does not encourage the left leg to accept the transfer of weight in the crosslateral move. It is easier to rotate. Practicing a weight shift will soon take the quiver out of the ankle. Shift onto the left leg and stand in balance for about ten seconds at a time. Do it as often as you can for about three months. This will remove the quiver.

Once a well-known pro broke his ankle, and it left him with a bit of restriction in the joint. Outlining the Joe Norwood crosslateral move as a substitute for his accustomed rotating with his knees and ankles brought forth this reply: The playing pros would have already discovered this move and would be using it, if it were any good. Surely, he should have been aware that the playing pros have, if not more, certainly deeper problems than your average hacker. It becomes hard to equate his statement with the hard facts as borne out by the tour players.

Too many golfers retain the balance of weight on the left side and thus don't get the right side into the shot. Stand behind a good golfer and watch the ball between his feet. As the forward swing is made, the right knee covers the ball as his right side shifts with the swing. It is possible to move the left side into the shot without having moved the right side into it. The driving power of the right leg is left out of the move.

Don't try to be a contortionist by trying to keep the head anchored during the swing. When the right side goes through, everything moves. Talk about whiplash! It is amazing how many people punish themselves by trying to swing while keeping the head still. Everything moves with the shot—head, chin, neck, body, and legs.

Pitcher Doug Rau, who threw his first major-league shutout recently at Houston, is quoted in an article in the Los Angeles *Times* as saying the following: "Pitching is not really complicated. It's like a golf swing. The easiest way to do it is to step into the direction you are aiming and use a motion that gives you maximum speed and power." Joe Norwood has been advocating this for many years. He is quite a student of baseball. He is always demonstrating this very idea of stepping into the box and not the bucket. There is a golf-o-metric for this exercise.

The bucket or the box? An exercise to encourage the left leg to take the weight transfer is to copy a baseball player when he steps into a pitched ball. Place the feet together, break both knees, and at the count of one step off with the left foot at about a forty-five-degree angle. At the count of two, step into the pitch; actually you shift onto the left leg while making the downswing at the same time. The arms should be at waist-high level, as a ballplayer using a bat. Great feelings of rhythm are derived from this exercise. Concentrate on the one-two-step, and the swing will come out by itself when the rhythm is developed. Naturally, this will be a bit awkward until the timing of the one-two-then-step-into-it routine becomes rhythmic. Spend a few minutes with this exercise. You will develop a rhythm and a loose-jointed, carefree swing. You will find the swing part of this exercise coming out by itself, a natural swing in effect. Don't stifle the swing by being stiff-legged, or rubbery, but use the legs with a definite pattern and purpose.

The left knee is the weakest point in the leg action. It is the counterpart of the left wrist. The left knee should be the No. 1 part to develop in teaching, but since everyone wants to hit the ball, it is of necessity last on the list of the four major parts. Not many people would be willing to spend three weeks learning how to get up on the left leg. The left leg must take the action of the right side delivering its power. It must resist the tendency to roll out and must learn to travel toward the big toe of the left foot.

The player is at the top of his swing, and the *sitz* is triggered off, and the right side delivers . . . whoosh . . . the crosslateral move is performed, and the player is onto his left leg in beautiful form. The arms have finished high and the left knee held the charge, and at the end of the follow-through he is over the big toe of the left foot. The right foot is canted inward, with about one row of spikes showing on the right side of the shoe. The weight shift has been completed. The move has been a down-and-forward move from underneath. No rotation or spinning out. The underneath feeling comes from the feeling of sitting on the right hip, sort of like a curtsy, which lowers the right buttock. Spinning out of the knees and ankles—in order to get the hips out of the way—has been avoided. The move is a relatively small one and yet affords a complete weight shift making the casual observer feel that no pivot took place. Now, and only now, is the golfer on the big toe of the right foot. This is where he gets the feeling that he pushed off on his big toe. The move by the right foot is inward; it cants inward toward the left foot. Getting up on the right toe isn't a power move. Instead of staying down through the shot, the toe dancer is coming up out of his shoes.

The validity of the crosslateral move can be readily proven by the following golf-o-metric. Assume the stance on the prop, place the butt end of the shaft under the left knee, and apply a backward pressure on the other end of the shaft, against the right leg, with the right hand. Try to rotate the left knee to the left side. The applied pressure holds the left knee inward and prevents it from rolling out, and this is the position and feeling the left knee should be in when the right side drives down to it: It is holding and accommodates the power of the right side. This is the strong-left-side feeling. Maintain the same address position and also the backward pressure with the club against the right leg, make the curtsy, go down and forward, and travel onto the left knee while keeping the left knee inward, inside the left instep of the left foot. You will find unrestricted movement; the legs and body are not blocked and are free to travel the normal distance onto the left leg—"onto" the left leg, and not "with" the leg. This automatically permits a longer follow-through with every shot. It permits the clubhead to stay on the ball longer. It allows complete freedom of action—no restrictions or blocking— and works this way on each and every shot, whether a drive or a putt.

The fizzled action of a window shade will be duplicated should the left knee go first in the downswing, the right leg following it. Should the right knee precede the downswing, the same will result. The knees must each play its part in holding and supporting. Each one takes its turn in proper sequence. Giving and taking is the game the knees play in a good, powerful golf swing.

"Climbing the wall"—this is the toughest golf-o-metric to perform, and not only for amateurs. This becomes a new experience for pros too, and quickly after hitting five or six balls in this manner they begin to feel some-

Crosslateral vs. rotating. Place the handle of the club to the inside of the left leg. Then pull the right hand backward, putting tension, which places the left knee and foot in a crosslateral position. Should the right hand and arm release the tension, the right side will rotate around the body, making a horizontal motion, known as outside-in, the opposite of the inside-out motion.

thing strange: They feel the ache of a new muscle being used for the first time. This exercise gets them on the right side of the short ribs. It helps them to power the ball, but it is a new experience for them. It is awkward to do, and no one will do it willingly. The exercise must be practiced with discipline, and more discipline.

"Climbing the wall" will help you to stay down on the insteps, shift the weight on the follow-through, and give the greatly desired high finish that only "Class A" golfers make and that looks so professional.

"Climbing the wall" encourages staying on the ball longer and permits the longest follow-through and the high finish. This describes what Lee Trevino does in his swing. Only the front part of the swing is used in this exercise. It goes from the address position along a straight line as far forward as possible and then up and above the head.

Place the toe of the clubhead against the wall of a house, or a fence, or a horizontal board. Lacking any of these, place a club on the ground and place the toe against the shaft, or scrape a straight line on the ground. What we are going to look for in this exercise is extension.

Take the address position and go forward with the clubhead, going as far as the crosslateral will allow, then follow the wall upward. Don't let the clubhead leave the wall. The hands must go above the head. The left wrist holds and the left elbow bends as the arms continue up and then around. Do not cut your neck off by leaving the wall and bringing the club around your neck. Cutting the neck off is the earmark of a rank amateur.

Repeat this exercise several times and you will get the feeling of chasing out after the ball "*à la* Lee Trevino." Being on the insteps is most apparent in this move, and it gets you onto the left leg. This is the feeling you should have after making each and every shot from the right side. Never leave your insteps during any shot—long or short, drive or a putt. The right foot is canted inward, with one row of spikes on the outside of the right shoe showing. Don't be a toe dancer; don't allow yourself to come up—stay down on the insteps of your feet. The move is very short and will give the impression that a pivot wasn't made and that little effort was expended in order to make the swing. You will look as effortless as Julius Boros.

To acquaint yourself with the curtsy, try this simple act. Assume the prop position and place your right hand on your right hip, or in your hip pocket, or on your hip pocket, whatever is most comfortable for you. Push down and forward with the butt of your palm, and you will feel yourself doing a bit of a curtsy. Try this a few times and get acquainted with this feeling, as it will become part of a necessary move. A variation of this is to place the hand on the hip again with the thumb on the back part of the hip and the fingers in front. Again, push down with the thumb and make the curtsy. Assume the same position one more time and pull yourself forward and around with a slight pressure from the thumb and fingers for the rotating move. You can always sample the two moves very easily by yourself. The curtsy will put you into the crosslateral, affording you the opportunity to make a strong swing at the ball instead of flailing at it while rotating.

Vertical vs. horizontal. Stand in an address
position. Then place the right thumb and
forefinger on the right hip. By pressing the
right thumb inward, the right side goes
crosslateral into the left knee and foot, which
lowers the right shoulder downward.

By comparison. By rotating the right index finger and the right shoulder, the hip goes around to the outside line, and anything can happen.

Synopsis of the Swing

The base of the swing is in your feet, which we call a "prop." It is a straight line of the right leg and foot with the knee slightly cracked. Sixty to 70 per cent of the weight is on the right side. The left knee drops in toward the ball, thereby reinforcing the right thigh. The prop, when complete, places the lower part of the body in a crosslateral position. The left arm is loaded with the left wrist setting down, becoming concave, and forcing the left thumb and forefinger up. The left arm will swing from the apex of the left shoulder. The right thumb and forefinger are sealed by the right wrist pressing inward and down, hooding the face of the club. The package of the thumb, forefinger, and wrist, acting as a unit, continues downward, while the right elbow and forearm swing to a horizontal position, which is the end of the backswing made with the hands and arms. The right thumb and forefinger is in a vertical position at this point. The backswing has gone into the right shoulder, which then lowers the left shoulder. This is where the pivot takes place, with the shoulders and not with the legs. Start the downswing with a vertical move out of the right shoulder and elbow in the direction of the right hip and heel, while the left arm remains loaded and extended. This allows the right arm to straighten, and the knees move crosslaterally, forcing the weight to the big toe of the left foot and allowing the right arm to continue on the line of flight and upward, an action only displayed by first-class golfers. If the left knee goes around it won't permit the club to go out straight; it changes the plane.

The straight line is a very confusing point in the golf swing to many. As you cross the line of flight you think your clubhead has to be squared; it already is, and in trying to square it again, you break the circle of the downswing and go to the ball instead of continuing the arc of the swing. If the hands remain tight, as in the address position, and the wrists are held firm, the blade will be held squared throughout the entire swing. When impact is made, the end of the arc is reached, and then the blade continues on a straight line until the end of the follow-through. The follow-through will vary with the amount of extension out of the right arm plus the amount of travel the legs make in the crosslateral. Some golfers will only extend the right arm an inch or two, and will only travel on the left knee an inch or two, and will then go around. Lee Trevino will travel a distance of approximately five to twelve inches with his irons and more with a wood. Extension does not cost any more effort than is already put into the swing; it is a matter of not quitting so soon and taking advantage of the action allowed.

The left side is torqued and is so powerful at the top of the swing it wants to lower itself, which is a pulling action, but you must retain the power in the left arm while the right arm is going downward to meet it, and then they go together. Power against power means explosive compression.

If the left knee or arm turns, you will go around the ball in a horizontal plane instead of a vertical one. Bypassing the vertical is the easy part of the swing; the hardest part of the entire swing is to make the vertical. Although the vertical move is only a fraction of an inch, it is merely the starter, but it can't be bypassed. It is the smallest move in the swing and the hardest to do. This is where Mr. Inside-out and Mr. Outside-in part company; this is the fork in the road. This is where more erroneous information about the golf swing takes place than in any other area, or part of the swing. Utter confusion. You cannot cross the line of flight on the backswing if you remain on the prop and do not rotate, with the right side dropped into its proper position. Get the right side in the proper position, and the left side will stay with it. This is called co-ordination. (For more on the vertical move see Position Three.)

Left-hand grip, with thumb and forefinger forming a V pointing in the direction of the right shoulder. Left arm extended and loaded from the left shoulder. The right thumb and forefinger forming a V pointing in the direction of the left side of the chin. This is due to the combination of the knuckle of the right forefinger and the right wrist turning inward, which give a hooded and awkward feeling during the adjustment.

Worth trying: a flexed right elbow. The right leg in a straight-line position from the knee to the foot. A backward press with the left knee places the right hip in a propped position, making 70 per cent weight on the right leg and 30 per cent weight on the left leg. This eliminates any extra body motion during the backswing.

The flexed right elbow initiates the starting of the backswing. The right thumb, forefinger, wrist, and forearm are in a circular motion in the direction of the right elbow, which is in a flat and horizontal position close to the right hip. The right thumb, forefinger, and wrist are pulling in a clockwise position, while the forearm and elbow are parallel to the ground. The entire left hand, wrist, and arm are in a vertical and outward position. The right leg and hip are propped, while the legs remain in a crosslateral position. Weight and position of the left leg show a slight change due to the left shoulder in a downward position over the ball.

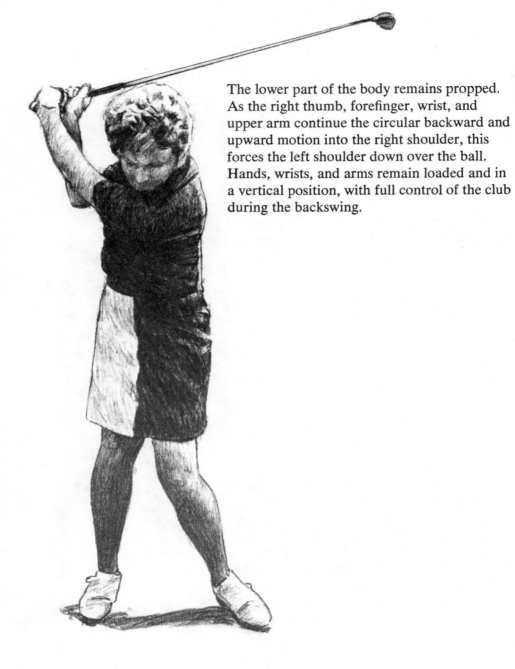

The lower part of the body remains propped. As the right thumb, forefinger, wrist, and upper arm continue the circular backward and upward motion into the right shoulder, this forces the left shoulder down over the ball. Hands, wrists, and arms remain loaded and in a vertical position, with full control of the club during the backswing.

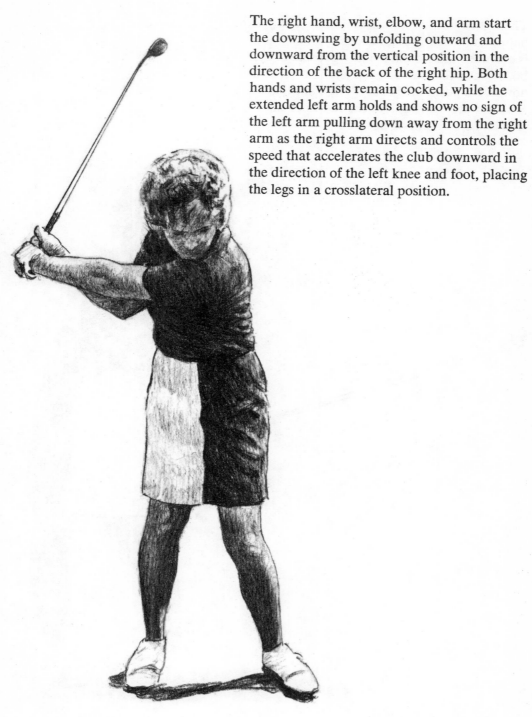

The right hand, wrist, elbow, and arm start the downswing by unfolding outward and downward from the vertical position in the direction of the back of the right hip. Both hands and wrists remain cocked, while the extended left arm holds and shows no sign of the left arm pulling down away from the right arm as the right arm directs and controls the speed that accelerates the club downward in the direction of the left knee and foot, placing the legs in a crosslateral position.

The right elbow continues to unfold. The
hands and wrists are still cocked. The left arm
is extended and holding. The right side of the
body shows the club delayed and in a vertical
downward position. The right hip, knee, and
shoulder are moving into the left knee and
foot in the crosslateral position.

As the right elbow and arm straighten against the extended left arm and left knee and foot, the right hand and wrist remain as part of the arm, as the speed of the right elbow and arm enters into the hitting area. The right arm has lowered the right shoulder, hip, and leg into the left knee and foot, which prevents any turn of the lower part of the body. The result is a straight ball with any club from this position.

The right elbow and arm continue through
the hitting area. The entire right side is down
under and out, while the hands, wrists, arms,
and club continue into the left knee and foot,
which is holding, while the hands, wrists, and
arms show no departure during the
straight-line position.

The follow-through shows the continuation of
the entire right side going out and up while
the left knee, foot, and side hold. This allows
the hands, wrists, and arms to hold the club as
the arms go into a high finish with no loss of
control from start to finish. This is seen only
in good golf.

Position One

Position One is the backswing that ends when the right forearm reaches a horizontal position. Anything higher than the parallel, or horizontal is a lift, and there is no centrifugal force in a lift. Joe's swing is comprised of two half circles, one going back and one returning. The backswing with the forearm position at the horizontal, or Position One, is nine feet long. The complete backswing is about twelve feet. Joe operates from a small hub that creates a great arc and a tremendous amount of centrifugal force.

The advocates of straight back from the ball and then the lift to achieve the high arc are many, but there is no centrifugal force in going back from the ball in a straight line, nor in a lift. Going back from the ball is a "carry," and the lifting action is comparable to it, as there is no arc or circle involved in either move. Any part of a circle will create swing force, and Joe's swing is made up of two half circles.

A simple way of making the backswing to Position One is to place the hands palm to palm and then lace the fingers together. Extend the left arm out of the shoulder and take the right forearm to a horizontal position that is about waist high. At no time does the forearm go beyond the horizontal position on the backswing. The elbow travels in a flat perimeter, and the flatter the elbow travels the more the right shoulder gets into the swing, building up centrifugal force.

To practice Position One, take a golf ball and place the thumb and forefinger on it as outlined in the chapter covering the grip, set the wrist down, and take it back, making the elbow circle your rib cage. There is no limit as to how many times a day you can or should practice this exercise. The more you do it, the more supple your elbow will become. The more you perform this move, the easier it will be to make your thumb become your boss. It is impossible to make the circle around the rib cage too tight with the elbow, and the more you force the elbow around with the thumb and forefinger the more centrifugal force you will develop in the clubhead. The thumb chases the index finger, so this will give you the opportunity of squeezing the ball while going to Position One, thereby allowing you to practice two golf-o-metrics at the same time.

There are many ways to start the backswing, and Joe knows them all. He offers one that is exquisite in that it begins with the smallest dimension. The hand or grip is already set in a circle, and when there are no changes made in the setup, the activation of the thumb and forefinger combined with the sealed wrist automatically go into a circular move, as the elbow is already open. The toe of the clubhead is the first thing that should start back, and the heel of the clubhead is the first thing that should start down. Straight back does not move the clubhead one iota. Watch it as it goes straight back; it is strictly a carry, then it goes into a lift, and by the time it is waist high, or higher, it hasn't gone into any part of an arc. Actually, it hasn't moved back in relation to the address position.

Joe's first move is nine feet, and it goes into a half circle, developing pure centrifugal force, by contrast to the straight-back-and-lift action. His wrist is set, or cocked at the maximum in the address position, and the built-in circle sets the clubhead flying from the very start. Speaking of starts, Joe starts the backswing from a dead start. Those who need to waggle had better learn to waggle with the arms and not with the hands, since you will swing as you waggle. Learn to waggle with the arms and not with the hands, and learn to make a complete waggle by going to Position One; the forearm must be in a horizontal position—not partially there, but fully horizontal. The thumb and forefinger of the right hand will be in a vertical position. Most golfers will only make a halfhearted effort to get to the horizontal position, and this will not crank the arm into the shoulder, and no benefits will be derived. The bad habit of lifting is hard to overcome.

The right side is made up of two parts, two moving parts—the wrist and the elbow. The action is the thumb and forefinger to the elbow via the seal of the wrist, and the elbow to the shoulder. The forearm travels to a horizontal position, while the elbow is traveling in a flat perimeter around the rib cage to Position One. One very important point to remember is that the thumb and forefinger must be put into Position One; it won't get there by itself. The thumb and forefinger go back to get up, and not up to get back. Let the thumb chase the index finger; don't lift to get back. This is where the flipping hands become active in the desire to toss the clubhead; hands and body go together—flipping and rotating are a team. Hands and wrists separate from the arms. The hand has no privilege when the seal of the wrist is retained. Retain the sealed wrist and use the arm. A supple elbow is necessary, and the need to practice going to Position One is a prime requisite.

The earmark of a Joe Norwood person is one who has a golf ball between the thumb and forefinger, squeezing and going to Position One, while in a courtroom, walking down the street, shopping in a supermarket, waiting for an elevator, *ad infinitum*. Practice, practice, practice.

Ted Winslow, a teaching pro at the West Los Angeles golf range, relates the following story, and it is so apropos to the importance of practicing Po-

Right-side control. The right leg in a straight-line position from the knee to the foot. A backward press with the left knee. Swinging the right thumb, forefinger, wrist, and arm backward and upward in a circular motion to the right shoulder. The right hand is holding the cocked position.

While the right arm unfolds downward and
vertical to the back of the right hip, the right
arm straightens, forcing the heel of the right
wrist to lower below the fingers of the left
hand, which has remained still. The move
allows the right shoulder to go down under at
contact.

By comparison. When the right thumb, forefinger, wrist, and arm are in a lifting motion, there is no circle, and anything can happen.

sition One. "About 1935 or 1937 Sam Snead was practicing for a local tourney in the Los Angeles area. He was hitting hundreds of balls a day with the sole purpose of perfecting his backswing. He wanted it so perfect that he no longer would have to think about it." Evidently the so-called natural swing was acquired. All good movements must be practiced in order to be acquired, so that they become second nature. With or without a ball, set up the thumb and forefinger and go to Position One as many times a day as you can. Develop the thumb and forefinger control and the fluidness of the elbow.

Imprint this in your memory. The thumb chases the index finger. It is thumb to finger on the backswing, with the wrist sealed, of course.

It took Joe ten years to find that the elbow went into the shoulder.

The shaft of the club is behind the hands in Position One. This requires a straight left hand and forearm, not a concave wrist.

Start the swing with about the same amount of effort that turning a key in an ignition switch requires. Start up the engine at an idling speed and not full throttle. Toss the clubhead nice and easy. Torquing the neck, shoulders, and body in a rigid manner and putting forth enough effort to hurl a piano twenty yards won't produce any results out of a twelve-ounce club.

Swallow a bit of pride, get off the ego trip, and leave the driver in the clothes closet. Play with a three-wood; it will give the same carry and less roll, but it will keep the ball in play. Handle it as lightly as you would a short chip shot. Pick a spot about sixty yards out and in your feelings swing for that distance from Position One. It will probably turn out to be the lightest, most effortless swing ever, and will have crunched the ball with applied compression. Swing all of the clubs with the same idea of swinging for sixty yards, in your feelings, and enjoy the controlled hit.

Review: Setting the wrist down to seal it puts the index finger higher than the thumb. The wrist is canted inward, and it puts the dimple at the base of the thumb in the eleven-o'clock position. This is the strongest position the hand can be in, and this action hoods the face of the clubhead. The wrist is in a neutral position when the dimple is at twelve o'clock. The forearm swings in a horizontal position; the thumb and forefinger and wrist rise in a vertical position. This is the end of Position One. The arms do not go above the horizontal position during any swing when you are on your right side. Know where the dimple is, and you know where your clubhead is at all times. Swing to Position One and maintain the cocked wrist in the eleven-o'clock position during the swing.

Position One is very short in feeling. You are operating from a small hub, but remember it has a long arc. In an actual full swing the clubhead will pass the left side of the head, and you will swear that the club did not get to vertical, because the feeling is so short. Put the sun to your back and take a swing while watching your shadow. Incidentally, this is Joe's private camera: It takes the best pictures and gives instant replays. Use his camera often to check yourself in the various positions. In your desire to further the swing because you feel it is too short, you will add a lift to it, and by doing so you will miss the vertical, or the up part of the backswing. Be content to know that Position One is all the distance the hands and arms need to travel. Position Two will reaffirm this fact. In an actual swing everything becomes furthered during the fluid motion of the swing. The hand goes back a bit more, the elbow goes around more, the arm folds more, and the combination of the shoulders and left knee will give you another three feet of arc. For the time being stay with Position One until you have developed all of its wonderful benefits.

When the wrists are high the backswing is sort of "woody" or stiff, and they go into a carry more readily. The wrists are to be set down; then the backswing becomes more fluid, lighter in feeling, and generates more centrifugal force as it moves freer and faster.

The more perpendicular the club is held, the more drag is felt. The desire to lift, yank, put more effort into it with the body becomes more apparent when the clubhead is on the ground, and as the clubs become longer. Practice balls teed up are more forgiving, are more tolerant of variations introduced, and require less effort. To overcome these handicaps Joe would like to teach golf from twenty-inch-high tees. Here is another of Joe's golf-o-metrics. Reverse the club and take the address position with the end of the shaft out in front of you about waist high, and make a backswing. Notice how free and easy this movement is, how rhythmic and how light in feeling. It requires absolutely no effort. Now do a complete swing from start to finish from an imaginary twenty-inch tee. This results in lots of rhythm, a tremendous amount of speed (you can hear the shaft whistle), and on the downswing the move was made inside-out. Reverse the club and swing from the twenty-inch tee as before, and the results are the same again, except you are swinging about five ounces more than when the shaft was reversed.

Swinging from a twenty-inch tee gives you the liberty to swing down and below the hips instead of around the hips. You won't swing outside-in from the twenty-inch tee. Note: This is called "the airline," and more of it is described in the chapter covering Position Three. Place the clubhead on the ground, and immediately the shoulders yank at the club as if it weighed twelve pounds instead of twelve ounces. The body retards the rhythm of the swing, pure effort goes into the act, and the light feeling, the speed, fast enough to make the shaft whistle, is gone. Were you to swing the clubhead with that speed you would no doubt drive the ball three hundred yards without trying. Introduce the body, and all of the goodies evaporate. Rhythm without effort is what Joe teaches. He would have everyone hitting off tees for one year. It reduces the effort and promotes easier learning of the swing. The takeaway from the ball should be as light as it is from a twenty-inch tee. Reverse the club and swing from the twenty-inch tee. Listen to the shaft whistle, feel the rhythm, and with no effort. Joe dares you to swing at a ball in the same easy, effortless, and rhythmic way.

Develop good practice habits. Remember to waggle with the arms and to go to Position One with that arm waggle, back to the ball, and then make your backswing to Position One and smack it.

Swinging the handle. Body position at the address is as usual. Left arm straight and right elbow flexed. Raise the handle about ten inches off the ground while practicing. This makes swinging the handle to Position One smoother and with less effort for the downward swing, producing a lighter feeling. Worth trying.

The holding power of the left arm, the grip with the right thumb and forefinger and wrist are usually lost when held too long. Once there is any release in any of the parts, a completely new grip must be taken. When practicing, renew the left-arm extension and the right-hand grip after each shot. Don't rake another ball toward you while retaining the grip from the previous shot. Many golfers are prone to hit ten to fifteen shots with the same grip; they just keep raking with both hands on the club. Renew the extension and grip with each and every shot.

Start each practice session with the following routine. Place both feet together, bend the knees, and have the knees and ankles touching. Now swing with the arms to and from Position One. Once you have developed a bit of rhythm from this stance you will find that you will be able to fly the ball to about 90 per cent of your potential. This will prove to you that a quiet body will enable you to make better and easier contact with the ball. It will also prove to your satisfaction that the gyrations of the legs and body won't add another 10 per cent in distance to the shot. Once you realize how detrimental body movement and effort are in making a smooth swing, you will more readily develop tempo, rhythm, and control. This is how and where you will develop confidence. Be good to yourself, give yourself a chance to make a swing with fewer wavelengths: It will breed confidence only because you are getting to own your swing through control.

Start the clubhead with a light toss from the thumb and forefinger sealed by the setting of the wrist. Don't try to steer the clubhead, or to make a circle, as it is already built in and working for you. The instantaneous start of the hand/wrist/elbow into a circle becomes a smooth swinging action, and the tighter the circle becomes the more centrifugal force is generated.

The wide arc is assured from the extended left arm, but the radius of the right traveling in its circle seems short in feeling. Do not try to lift after you get to Position One. The horizontal position with the forearm is as high as it should be; don't try to further the arc. You will cross the line of flight by doing this and lose the Norwood track. A tiny gear is used to start a large one. Use the small dimension of the thumb and forefinger to start the wide arc of the clubhead slowly and lightly, just as that small gear will start a large one. Most golfers operate from the elbows down, and the tremendous power of the arms and shoulders above the elbows is unused. Learn to swing with the arms.

Golf would be easy if the clubhead were tossed in the same manner that an expert fisherman tosses a fly. Most golfers make the same moves but in the opposite sequence. Golf would be easy for the average golfer were he to reverse his procedure. Were the average golfer to start the downswing as he starts his backswing, he would have it made. Instead of hand/forearm to arm and shoulder, he starts with the shoulders, and on the down, he starts with the hand.

The powerful thrust out of the shoulder first is lost, as the hand will not take out the arm and shoulder. It is a one . . . two . . . three . . . move. But Mr. Average Golfer makes it out to be three . . . two . . . one. It is a

The circle. Keep the right thumb, forefinger, wrist, and elbow moving clockwise by pushing the right hand and arm downward opposite the right knee. From this position the right hand and wrist never pass the straight right arm while it continues along the line of flight. The right shoulder lowers, following the right arm outward and upward after contact.

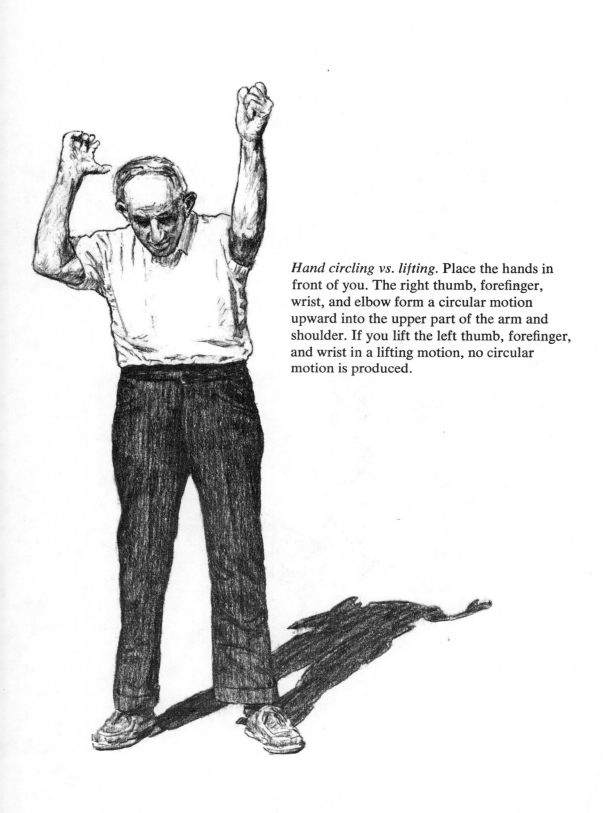

Hand circling vs. lifting. Place the hands in front of you. The right thumb, forefinger, wrist, and elbow form a circular motion upward into the upper part of the arm and shoulder. If you lift the left thumb, forefinger, and wrist in a lifting motion, no circular motion is produced.

toss from the hand/wrist and not a yank with the shoulders. Even a novice carpenter uses a hammer in the proper sequence; it is the only way to use it effectively. The golf swing sequence is the very same as it is in a hammer blow. The arm is used in making the swing with the hammer and not the hand. Using the hand to strike a tiny nailhead would be a pretty frustrating experience, as it is in a golf swing. Use the arm by retaining the hand.

The easiest and fastest way to learn the moves involved in making the Joe Norwood swing is to practice swinging from Position One. The name of the game as far as Joe is concerned is control. It is far easier to control a nine-foot swing from Position One than a twelve-foot swing from Position Two.

Take a trial swing to Position One, return the clubhead to the address position, make the backswing to Position One again, and then make the downswing. The trial swing and then the actual swing will give you a greater feeling of what you are doing and where you are, and you will find yourself swinging with greater ease and stroking the ball on a straight line.

Develop the control so necessary, and the transition from Position One to Position Two will come easily and naturally.

Stand steady, toss the hand/wrist/forearm to the right shoulder, and then use the right shoulder to power the downward thrust. Using the right shoulder means coming out of the shoulder—thrusting out of the shoulder, not turning the shoulder/torso in a twisting action. Don't use the body and shoulder to yank and hoist a twelve-ounce club. Using the proper parts and muscles will allow you to finesse the move easily, rhythmically, and gracefully.

Remember: The forearm goes to parallel only; anything below that won't allow the arm to crank into the shoulder, and above parallel goes into a lift bypassing the arm into the shoulder action. The powerful drawn feeling of the forearm is lost also when this part of the move is bypassed. The activator, which is the thumb/forefinger, is constant—it is always in motion and must go back to get up.

Put the waggle into the elbow and put the club in Position One and you won't labor.

Don't play the ball. Play the swing.

Position Two

Basically, Position Two is from the waist to the top of the backswing. The clubhead travels approximately twelve feet in a full backswing, of which about nine feet is covered by Position One, leaving about three feet for Position Two.

Previously it was said that Joe's swing was comprised of two half circles, and Position Two introduces the vertical. This may hold the interest of those who were turned off by the statements of the forearm swinging on a horizontal plane; actually it is the elbow that swings on a flat plane.

The combination of the thumb/forefinger/wrist and elbow has put your right arm in Position One. It went "back" to this point, and now it is going to go "up." To repeat a Joe Norwoodism: "Go back to get up, not up to get back." In the back of the right shoulder there is a booster muscle; when the thumb/forefinger does its job and gets back far enough it will trigger the booster muscle in the shoulder, and the vertical action will take place. This is where the arm goes into the shoulder. This is what is so beautiful about this move; it is a guaranteed package. Using the elbow to get back will put the arm into the shoulder, and the right shoulder will force the left shoulder down.

The left knee can be a blocker to this action. Upon taking the prop position, the left knee is tucked inward. This becomes the gateway for the lowering of the left shoulder, but it is also a teammate of the right arm and furthers it, allowing it to go back and into the right shoulder. When the player holds the left knee rigid he retards the shoulder action. The left shoulder stays high; the right arm doesn't get back. Many golfers have the left knee pointing either to their left or straight ahead and also use it to get up on during the backswing. With this action the shoulders are prevented from going into Position Two. The backswing is then incomplete.

A one-inch inward move from the left knee, combined with the shoulder action, will kick the clubhead another three feet, completing the twelve-foot

Body and shoulder. A rocker-arm position. Place the club across the shoulder. Then push—don't pull—the left hand and arm downward, placing the left shoulder in a vertical position, with the right leg and hip prop allowing the right hand, wrist, and arm to continue back and up into the right shoulder.

The pressure remains in the shoulders, while
the right hand, wrist, and arm push downward
in a reverse vertical move. This provides the
crosslateral motion into the left knee and foot,
which keeps you back of the ball.

backswing. The hands and arms in themselves never went above the parallel position. The shoulders pivoted, or operated in a pulleylike fashion. The massive arms and shoulders were used in making the backswing effortlessly instead of laboring with the uncertain action of flippy hands. The shoulders make an extended move—Joe calls it a rocker-arm motion; they produce tremendous power with little effort. Most golfers turn their shoulders in a flat plane, or twist them back and forth by torquing the torso. Twist on the backswing and you will untwist on the downswing. A twist will only produce an outside-in action. You wouldn't try to operate a set of pulleys by twisting to the left and then to the right. You would pull them alternately from the shoulders. Turning and twisting the shoulders on a flat plane move them from wall to wall. A pulley action with the shoulders will move them from floor to ceiling, east to west, or north to south, whatever will give you a clearer idea of what takes place. The shoulders moving on a flat plane will produce slices and hooks, as it is a rotating movement.

Stand in front of a mirror, or watch your reflection in a window, or better yet, use Joe's "camera." Take the stance in the address position, go to Position One and hold it, note where the clubhead is, drop the left knee inward, and watch the clubhead jump another three feet. Three feet of additional arc out of a one-inch move with the left knee and with no added effort. Better yet, trigger the booster muscle and it kicks like a mule, and this too without any further effort, all the result of harnessing the heavy muscles. The shoulder muscles that can put a heave-ho into a piano are certainly a match for a twelve-ounce club. Joe can hit a bucket of balls on a hot day and not perspire. He has trained his muscles to work for him, and he doesn't have to labor.

Here's a golf-o-metric to test your very own booster muscle: Without a club, set your right hand into the grip position out in front of you, preferably in a parallel-to-the-ground attitude. Place the tips of the fingers of the left hand on the right shoulder blade. Take the right hand straight back from an imaginary ball, then up, as you would in a golf swing. You will not feel anything happen in the shoulder-blade area. Resume the position again, and this time swing the right arm back into Position One: Now you feel the muscles bunching up from this action. One feeling is empty, and the other is loaded with power. The empty feeling won't give you the rocker-arm action and certainly not the explosion of power from that booster muscle. Go back to get up, not up to get back.

Action and reaction. Shoulders moving east and west will take you around the ball, and shoulders going north and south will take you down and through the ball.

Eventually Position One and Position Two blend and become a single move in feeling. The move is very short, and there is no awareness of having to make a second move. You will miss, or skip, the vertical when you lift and don't get that elbow back around your rib cage. The thumb-and-forefinger combination must go to its maximum position each and every time. You cannot become complacent about this move, as it will never get

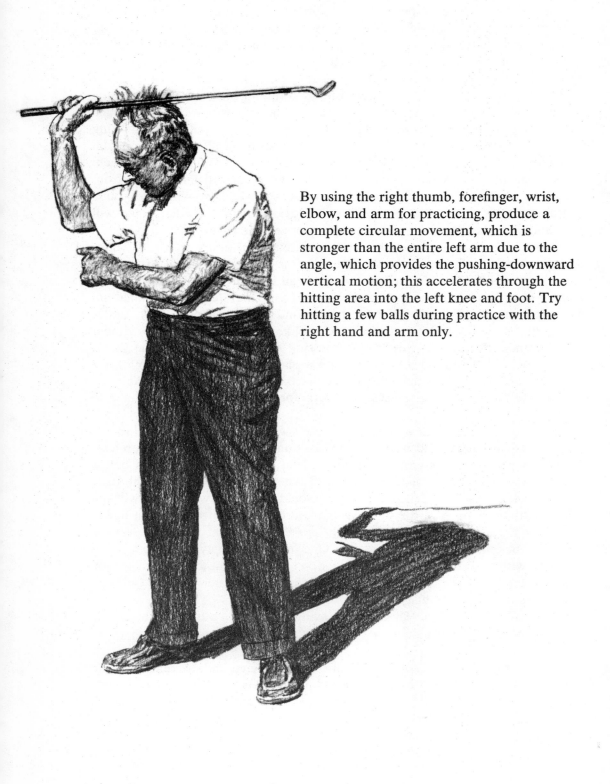

By using the right thumb, forefinger, wrist, elbow, and arm for practicing, produce a complete circular movement, which is stronger than the entire left arm due to the angle, which provides the pushing-downward vertical motion; this accelerates through the hitting area into the left knee and foot. Try hitting a few balls during practice with the right hand and arm only.

By comparison. Now compare the most common fault, which shows the dropping and lowering right elbow, allowing the left side to rotate to produce an outside motion to the ball.

back there by itself—you must put it there. Get that thumb, forefinger, and elbow back far enough to trigger the booster muscles and you will unleash power you never dreamed you were capable of producing.

The right side has been operating from a small hub throughout all of this action. The extended left arm travels in an outside line creating the longest arc possible. Most players take the club back on an inside line instead of an outside line. Here is a golf-o-metric that is self-explanatory when demonstrated. Extend the right arm out directly in front of yourself, extend the index finger, swing it back to Position One, and hold. Extend the index finger of the left hand and swing the arm toward the right, trying to touch the index finger of the right hand. Unless you first extend the left arm from the shoulders and allow the left arm to travel in an outside line, you won't be able to touch the right index finger with the left index finger. In the stretch to make contact with the right index finger you feel a pull in the left shoulder, and this is the feeling golfers get in making the backswing with an extended left arm, and the reason they think they are pulling with the left. This is why most think the golf swing is made by pulling.

Place your right hand over your left shoulder blade, and the fingertips will feel the extensor muscle working as you extend and release the left arm. It is possible to extend this muscle five to seven inches, but only a Hogan or a Trevino, as examples, can muster the holding power to retain this much extension. There are a lot of good left arms on the tour, and only two are mentioned. These two have proven without a doubt that they own a straight line when striking the ball. Develop the holding power to support a one- or two-inch extension, and your only problem will be your short game, because you neglected giving it the time it deserved.

The golf-o-metric to develop the holding power in the left arm can be done at any time, in any place, and as many times a day as one wishes. No club is necessary; just extend the arm and carry it across your body and hold it for ten seconds.

A simple golf-o-metric that will train your elbow to travel around your rib cage follows: Hold a club by the shaft with the left hand just above the clubhead, and with the right elbow at the side and forearm parallel. Place the shaft in the crook of the right elbow, and set the thumb, forefinger, and wrist into the grip position. The shaft will be in about a forty-five-degree angle. Activate the thumb, push the index finger, and watch the elbow travel around your rib cage as it follows the shaft.

Starting a backswing straight back from the ball will not force your elbow into this circular move. Going straight back will produce a "carry," and the elbow will leave your body. Some call it a flying elbow. There isn't any centrifugal force in this type of move.

Starting the backswing with shoulders and/or body will give you the same result. Pulling the arm around the body will produce zero centrifugal force also. Push the thumb against the index finger to initiate the circular move that creates centrifugal force.

The rotor on a helicopter is powered by a small gear. This tiny source of power operates the huge rotor blades, and they appear to be circling lazily, but such tremendous centrifugal force is generated by the rotor tips that about one thousand horsepower of stored energy is developed. Looking for power without effort in the golf swing? Why not use the same principle of a tiny motor generating a thousand horsepower? Why not use the elbow as a tiny hub that generates so much centrifugal force so easily? Nature designed the elbow in such a way that it is impossible to roll it by itself. It is completely dependable. Were you to trust the move that the elbow makes you would be able to hit a ball blindfolded—on purpose and straight, too.

Of course, there is a right way and a wrong way, as in all things. A lifting action at this point will nullify the wanted action. The arms will fold in a lift, and all of the stored energy in the arms and shoulders will be released. The vertical will be skipped also. This action is likened to an archer and his bow. The archer's left arm holds, the right arm draws back the bowstring, everything is taut. Should the left arm release at this point, all of the energy dissipates, and the bowstring becomes a limp element. A release of the golfer's left arm, or the folding of the right arm, will duplicate the action just described. The right arm must get back to get up, and a lift will undo the dynamic tension that is built into the move.

Put the thumb/forefinger back, and Joe guarantees the package of getting the arm cranked into the shoulder, which in turn will trigger the booster muscle, and the thumb/forefinger will rise vertically. This tiny move will deliver another three feet of arc free of charge. It requires no further expenditure of effort.

Operating from the small hub of the elbow will give you a feeling of shortness in the swing. This of course is false, and the golfer should refrain from giving it an added lift at this point. When the riser goes into action and kicks the clubhead three feet it will go past the left side of the golfer's head. Use Joe's camera, the sun, and watch your shadow on the ground. Make a full swing and see the clubhead pass the left side of your head, proving that the shortness in feeling is misleading and that you are getting a full twelve feet of arc.

Browse through the old golf magazines and find a picture of Ben Hogan in Position Two. You will see the tautness of the energized extended left arm, the convex wrist, the curl in the hand made by the tightening of the pinky finger. Dynamic energy seems to flow from that holding left arm, fully extended. He is in good balance and ready to pounce on the ball. All he need do at this point is make the vertical in reverse. This move is the smallest, the tiniest move in the entire golf swing to make. This is where good golf and bad golf meet the fork in the road.

Evidently Joe teaches much of what Sam Snead and Lee Trevino also do as revealed by pictures of them in action. The classic positions of Hogan, Snead, and Trevino bear out the basic fundamentals as described herein. It is amazing to see the almost identical similarities of Snead and Trevino in recent pictures. Fantastic left arms extending out of the shoulders, straight left wrists, or flat, the legs temporarily bowed as if they were riding broncos,

Straight left hand, wrist, and arm. A good
prop position. Right thumb, forefinger, wrist,
elbow, and arm in a swinging position. To
further the swing, the right hand and arm pull
backward and upward into the right shoulder.
The power and position are left out by 70 per
cent of all golfers.

a result of the *sitz,* that momentary jump at the ball before going into the crosslateral move. Analyzing the pictures makes it understandable why these golfers became so great.

This is the end of Position Two, no less and no more. Do not lift; go back to get up.

Position Three

The basic part of the golf swing in Position Three is from the top of the backswing down to the waist, or parallel position of the forearm.

The start of the downswing is the smallest unit in golf. It is so tiny it is very hard to measure. It is elusive and very hard to perform. It is the finest point in the swing. It can be called a perpendicular move, but Joe calls it a vertical move. Trackwise, the last inch up is the first inch down. By the numbers, it is 1-2-3-4, and reversing, 4-3-2-1. The ball is hit on the first inch of the downswing. It is the cause, and everything else that follows is the effect. The first effort down cannot be nullified or recalled; you are committed. The first inch down is either a pull or a swing. This is where the golfer stays behind the ball or goes around it. A baseball pitcher's arm is the best example of the elbow coming out first with the hand retained. Photographers like to take pictures of this piece of action. It is dynamic and a very awkward-looking action. The move is a push or a thrust, not a pull. A pitcher never throws with his hand. He uses his arm, and pictures reveal this so clearly. A golfer must do the same—hit the ball with the arm and not with the club. Use the arm to bring the club down; otherwise the wrist will do it, and then the hand flips. The No. 1 error in golf is the body going first and not the arm. The "chuck" out of the elbow is the key point in making the downswing.

Golfers, are you ready for this? At the top of the backswing the very first move of the downswing is backward—yes, backward, and away from the ball. This is a mind-boggling statement, since the eye and the mind are focused on the ball out in front. The ball is a magnet. The anxiety level to hit it is always high. The need for discipline is great at this point of the swing. The desire is to hit the ball, and yet the first requisite is to make a backward move. Once that tiny backward move is made, it is all downhill. You are home free.

The elbow chucks out and downward and comes out of the shoulder as it continues. That tiny move out of the elbow, once started, goes off like a rocket. A move less than a quarter of an inch starts the powerful pistonlike arm and shoulder. Using the powerful arm and shoulder in the downswing is what makes the swing so effortless. A twelve-ounce club is no challenge to those husky members of the body. No wonder Julius Boros looks so cool when he swings.

Harry Vardon, according to Joe, would have a stake set in the ground at about a forty-five-degree angle behind him. From the top of his backswing Vardon would make an effort to hit that stake with his clubhead in trying to go back with the downswing. Vardon practiced hitting at a stake for hours at a time. He was never off a fairway in three years, says Joe. No doubt you have read similar observations of Vardon previously. It is said that each following day his ball would be in the divots he made the day before. Straight, straight, straight: This is what Joe Norwood is all about.

Fortunately for the golfer, there are only two ways to swing at a ball: One either swings around, or down and through, as it is in good golf. When one goes around he has missed the down, or vertical, and is going to the ball. It will result in a departure of the shoulders, arm, and hand. It is here that the shoulder rotates; the arm is lowered, or pulled, which in turn reduces the radius of the arc from 20 to 40 per cent. The hand is cast prematurely in conjunction, and all other errors become compounded. These departures are the result of a pull instead of a thrusting action from the elbow, missing the vertical. This is where the body goes around the ball before the swing is made; then the belated swing is made outside-in. The good golfer does not swing *around* his hips; he swings *under* his hips. The swing will then take the body. The speed out of the elbow is then magnified by the mass of the body being added to the swing.

Speed plus mass are what move a golf ball. Do not swing harder; merely swing faster. The faster the chuck is made out of the elbow, the more speed is developed. Everything else remains the same except for the added speed out of the elbow. A swing out of the elbow will take a two-hundred-pounder through the shot, but when a two-hundred-pounder tries to overpower a twelve-ounce club, the ball doesn't get very much flying time.

The way nature built the elbow it cannot be rolled by itself, only by the use of the arm. The elbow cannot oscillate, like a hand. It is dependable and will repeat the same move over and over until it wears itself out. It is like a punch press. A punch press has an instant release in order to generate velocity and deliver its Sunday punch. It doesn't loaf on the way down; it is compressive. This is the way that the swing should be made out of the elbow. Do not lower the elbow from the top of the swing. This is as bad as a pull from that position. The swing must start out of the elbow prior to any other move with any other member or part involved.

To illustrate this move, pick up a hammer and take it up to a position as if you were going to strike at a nail in a wall. The first move is a swing out of the elbow; the hand is retained. Repeat the backswing with the hammer, hold it at the top, and drop the elbow instead of swinging at the nail. This action is a pull. Pick up the hammer again, hold it aloft, bring it around to your side, and strike out at an imaginary nail from that position. The elbow swings straight out, as it does in a golf swing. Repeat the position and again lower the elbow as in a drop, and note the fact that the elbow did not unfold; this is what happens in a pull. The elbow does not become activated. Lowering the elbow does not change the dimension of the fold or cause the unfolding of the arm.

All parts of the swing are held, and nothing moves during the pause at the top of the swing. Hesitate for as long as you wish in this position. When the chuck out of the elbow takes place it triggers a series of actions. Pictures taken in slow motion would reveal the following: The right hip initiates the *sitz;* this is a sudden jolting move just like the action of a punch press, and it is only of a split-second duration. It is a very compressive move. In a split second all of the compression is on its way to the feet. The *sitz* is made from underneath. The right buttock is tucked under, and the feeling of a curtsy is in the action, and the feeling of sitting on the hip is also felt. As the curtsy is made, the torso does a slight backward tilt as the right shoulder goes down and under. The legs, being attached to the ground, give the feeling that the very first move in the downswing is from the feet. The legs, having a shorter distance to travel, do get to the ball first. The *sitz* permits the arms to swing while going into the crosslateral, but in a rotation it is very difficult to swing and rotate at the same time. Up to this point there have not been any departures or releases of the coiled power, the holding parts; nothing is wasted or dissipated. All compression is retained. The dynamic power of the arms and legs are delivering. "Pounds into the ground"—another Norwoodism. It merely means driving the "sitter" into the ground, creating more compression, pouncing on the ball, riding a bronco. Every move up to this point has been concise, nothing left to chance. There are no variations or departures to contend with, and the moves are dynamic. Without all of these disciplined moves the golfer is equipped with a lot of slack in his swing, and removing this slack bit by bit is Joe's biggest job—tightening up the swing, reducing the negatives on a priority basis, lessening the free-wheeling aspects of the average golfer.

At the top of the swing it is important that the flexors are not grabbing, and they will not if the elbow is flexed, open, relaxed, and moving fluidly. The right elbow must be in a fluid state at all times, in every shot and with each and every club, from a driver to a putter.

The left side is the taker; it is in a state of controlled power, dynamic tension supporting the torqued position of the arms and shoulders awaiting the explosive charge from the right side. The right side is the activator, and coordination takes place when the actions complement each other. This is true of the left and right arms, as they are separate in themselves but work together as a team. All muscles on the left side go down into the hand, and the muscles on the right side go up from the hand and forearm into the shoulder. The right side is generally left out of the swing because of the predominant feeling in the left side. We think that the left side dominates by feel,

Entire left hand, wrist, and arm extended and loaded from the left shoulder, rather than with the left shoulder. Body position remains propped and shows no sign of helping.

and think it will do all of the work, but it won't. Muscles must be pushed and not pulled. A throwing arm is a pushed action from the arm and shoulder. Rhythm is the right wrist and forearm moving an opened elbow. Legs and body won't move the arms.

A mental picture of all this seems to be incorporated in the actions of the village blacksmith. Picture the blacksmith holding a red-hot horseshoe in his tongs and resting the horseshoe on an anvil. He raises his right arm, hammer in hand, and swings at the horseshoe held on the anvil with his left arm. The left holds, it does not pull away. It stays put, and the right-handed blow is effective. These are all separate movements, and yet all are co-ordinated. In the golf swing most golfers are pulling their left arm away, and the right arm dissipates its power in trying to catch up to it. The action is power against power when the left arm is held and the right smacks against it, and it's a blow struck with authority. Just picture a charged-up left arm holding, not pulling, awaiting that powerhouse right arm.

The chuck from the elbow is an out-and-down move from the shoulder and arm. The right shoulder rocks, or tilts back, and a feeling of the thumb pushing the shaft over the index finger takes place as the elbow triggers the chucking action. The feeling of the shaft tipping over is a result of a previous action from the elbow and is not to be done voluntarily by using the thumb to accomplish this feeling. This is Joe's rocker-arm action, or shoulder pivot. The shoulders going north to south, floor to ceiling, and then reversing. It is a combination move, as it all happens together, with no delineation of the parts. Do not drop the elbow or pull with it. Whatever position the elbow is in at the top of the backswing is where the chucking action takes place.

There are two starters in the swing. One is at the address position, and the other is after the pause at the top of the backswing. The backswing from the ball is a half circle, and then it goes into its vertical. On the downswing it reverses itself, first the vertical and then the half circle. The pause is between the vertical rising and the vertical going down.

Many golfers just can't make the pause, since they swing in such a manner that they rebound from several inches to a foot after reaching the top of their swing. Lack of flexibility in the long thumb grip causes the rebound as well as the force in the backswing.

Take advantage of the greatest camera in the world, the sun. And watch the picture of your swing by the shadow cast. In executing Position Three you should see the clubhead leaving the back of your neck. In a swing out of the elbow you will see this happen. In a pull you will see it lowered. Notice the difference in the arc between these two moves. One has a great arc, and the pull has none worth mentioning. This is visual proof that a swing out of the elbow creates a great arc.

Watch your shadow reveal what happens when the vertical is skipped. The player goes to the ball and crosses the line of flight. The right arm must swing from the very top of the backswing, and this is where and how the elbow is kept close to the body. This is where and how the inside-out move originates. To repeat: Do not pull the arm toward the ball or drop the elbow from the peak of the backswing. Above all: Don't cast the hand toward the ball. Any departure at this point will ruin the swing. Any move that will break the arc will break the swing.

The shoulders work in a pulley fashion, seesaw, rock, or tilt. Holding the position at the top of the backswing, you can make the vertical move, both down and up, by trying to straighten the right arm just a fraction of an inch. This tiny move will cause the shoulders to respond and pivot from ceiling to floor and vice versa. Look behind you and notice the backward move the clubhead makes when you make the vertical downward. The downswing starts at the very point the backswing ends. Like a diamond cutter, who must strike a sharp blow, so must the golfer. The closer to starting the down after the finish of the backswing the sharper the blow will be, and the shot will be more accurate.

The top of the backswing finds the left side so powerful and the position so high that it wants to lower itself, which is pulling. You must retain the holding power of the left arm while the right goes to meet it, and then they both go together. Turning with the left knee at this point, or pulling with the left arm makes the swing horizontal instead of vertical, resulting in a roundhouse swing instead of down and through, with a squared clubface meeting the ball on a straight line. A roundhouse swing will meet the ball with a curving line, and the ball will respond accordingly.

The arms are independent but work together. This is a most important point. The desire to hit the ball is so great that the golfer breaks the circle and goes to the ball. He does not realize that if all of the parts are held, the clubface is already squared and will meet the ball in that squared position. He thinks he has to square it, and this is where he breaks the circle, or the bottom arc of Joe's swing.

The start of the downswing is a vertical move out of the shoulder and elbow in the direction of the right heel. The left arm remains loaded and extended, while the right arm straightens itself against it. The knees move crosslaterally, forcing the weight to the big toe of the left foot. This allows the right arm to continue on the line of flight and upward for the high finish. When the vertical is missed, rotation will take place and will not allow the club to go on a straight line at impact. Rotation encourages the club to cross the line of flight. Ninety per cent of the golfers do not put the right shoulder into the swing. For power crank up into the right shoulder and come out of the shoulder.

The left side should never get ahead of the ball. The left side must stay behind the ball.

When the left arm pulls first, the right arm can't catch up to it without using the hand to do so, and this spells big trouble. When the flipping right hand enters into the act, fearful happenings take place.

The left side is a holding side, and the right, which is the power side, goes to it in a strong, thrusting move. Should the left side go first, the right side will merely follow, and the thrusting power will have vanished.

Do not initiate the downswing by pulling with the left shoulder instead of going down with the right shoulder. It is most imperative that at this point in the swing the left must hold while the right arm smacks against it.

The start of the downswing predicates the swing pattern, and full commitment is made by the type of start made. It will be either horizontal or vertical. Miss the vertical on the downward stroke and you will go to the ball in a rotating movement. There is no turning back, no second chance to make a change in the swing pattern once the start has been made.

Make the down from the very top of the backswing or rotate toward the ball. Either swing or pull from this point.

During a practice session take a backswing and hold the position at the top of the swing, turn your head and look at your hands, start a downward thrust just a fraction of an inch, just barely enough to make the hands move. Do the hands move forward or do they move backward? If the hands moved forward it was because the starting move was initiated by a pull instead of a thrust, or push. Also, instead of going back to get up, the clubhead went up to get back. The thumb and forefinger were lazy, they did not force the elbow back far enough to trigger the booster muscle, which in turn would trigger the *riser,* or make the vertical move up. By going up, the forearm folded inward and released the dynamic tension that may have been set up at the address position. Getting the thumb and forefinger back far enough to trigger the almost automatic responses as just outlined will put the hands and club behind the shoulder with all of the dynamic tension cranked up into the arm and shoulder intact. Now comes the hard part, in fact it is the hardest part in the golf swing, period. The clubhead is at the extreme position of the backswing, and it is at this point that the diamond must be cleaved. Make that tiny thrust, just a fraction of an inch, and you will find that the hands start backward first before continuing the downward path. A quarter-inch move from this position can power a ball 150 yards with a driver. The tremendous power cranked into the arm and shoulder is fully utilized, there is no loss of power in this move. One might call it direct drive; no power is lost in transit, or transmission. The backward move is momentary and very short. Making the thrust, or push, from the very top of the backswing is really hard and will require a good deal of practice. This move is so minute it is no wonder that the golf swing has remained a mystery these many years. Thanks to Joe, it has been isolated and made known again. The mysterious move is no longer mysterious though; it seems to have become lost in the many translations since Harry Vardon's time.

Practice *à la* Harry Vardon, when at the top of the swing strike out at an imaginary stake just to the right and behind the right hip. Joe will guarantee that you will then return the heel of the clubhead first, insuring a proper swing plane, the inside-out move to the ball. Returning the toe of the clubhead first is the result of a pulling action, and this will guarantee an outside-in swing, incorrect swing plane, hooks and slices each and every time. Everyone can learn to make this vertical move down, male or female, young or old, tall or short, lean or fat; it doesn't even favor the strong over the weak. What matters most and counts most at this point is the speed in which the chuck, or first move out of the elbow, takes place. Generating clubhead speed is the final object. This is the source of cause, and everything that takes place after the first move out of the elbow is effect. Too much is made out of the effect in teaching and very little as to cause. Can you imagine what chance the average golfer has to make a good swing after being so instructed: stand loose, legs relaxed, light grip, turn your body, let the body take the arms and shoulders to the top of the backswing, release the hands near the bottom of the downswing, etc. The hands came in too early, the hands came in too late, all handy phrases that will cover any number of failures to make good contact but none of them telling the befuddled golfer what to do, and what to do it with, as does Joe Norwood through his golf-o-metrics. The downswing is so fast, once commitment from the top is made there is hardly a chance for anyone, let alone a rank amateur, to make changes or introduce additional movements into the downswing. Not unless one has been programmed like some exotic ballistic missile. Encouraging Mr. Average Golfer to supinate, or roll the hands over, after impact, following the instructions to release the hands at the bottom of the downswing, really is too much for anyone to handle.

All of these tricky goodies are end results of prior commitments as they must be executed before the actual contact is made. This places a very tight schedule on the golfer, as he can hardly think this fast, let alone execute this many compensating moves. The emphasis seems to be placed on compensations and developing a compensating swing instead of learning to simplify the Joe Norwood way. Why not teach specifics that will enable the golfer to learn what goes into the act and to learn to control his swing as a result of Joe Norwood's golf-o-metrics. Make the vertical move instead of the horizontal. The ability to make the vertical is based on the individual's level of experience, and this move is what separates good and bad golf. The vertical vs. the horizontal is what separates Joe Norwood's teachings of the golf swing from others.

Position Four

Technically speaking, Position Four is from the waist to the ball, as it is an extension, or continuation, of Position Three.

Hands and body will produce hooks and slices, whereas the teamwork of arms and legs produce effortless power, and the flight of the ball will be unbelievably straight.

The goal is to get to the point of impact with a loaded and holding left arm, the left wrist maintaining the convex setting; the right wrist is sealed with the dimple at the eleven-o'clock position, and the blade is squared and slightly hooded. For maximum effect, the right arm has made a full extension.

A release of the holding power of the left arm will result in a change of dimension; losing the convex wrist will cause a pull or a flip with the left hand. The clubhead will pass the hands. Releasing the seal of the right wrist will find the right hand overpowering the left, the right-arm extension that powers the ball will be nullified, and the golfer will be going around the ball instead of down and through the ball. Impact will be made with a curving blade and not one that is squared.

In good golf, the hands are always ahead of the clubhead. This assures getting to the ball with a squared blade, providing all parts are held and functioning.

The chuck-out of the right elbow is toward first base, and the left arm momentarily swings away from the body; it does not pull toward the target. Should the left arm pull, the right will dissipate its stored power chasing after the left. The chuck from the right elbow sends the swing down under the hips and not around the hips.

Opening or laying the right hand back will stop the right arm from continuing its thrust, and there will be a loss of follow-through, as the swing will then go around the player's neck instead of up and above the head. The eleven-o'clock position of the dimple on the right wrist must be held to prevent all of these happenings.

Assume the stance, or prop, on the right leg, and without the use of a club, extend the left arm, with the index finger pointing to the ground, as if an imaginary ball were teed up there. Set the right-hand grip, flex the elbow, and go to Position One, then Position Two. Going to Position Two will pull the index finger off the ball. Continue to watch the index finger of the left hand as you go to Position Three and Position Four. Should the left index finger return to the ball as you make the downswing, it is because the left arm isn't holding. The left arm is pulling, and the right arm has to chase after it. Had the left arm held the index finger in the same place after the right arm had gone to Position One, you would find yourself thrusting your right arm against a strong holding left arm. Power against power. Crunch!

An early left and a lazy right equal a "carry" and end in a pull, and this statement says everything that the previous paragraph outlined.

Once again, and without a club, assume the address position on your prop. Again, extend the left arm and index finger. Swing the right to Positions One, Two, Three, and Four. Note the pulley action of the shoulders as they go north to south, floor to ceiling, and reverse—not east to west or wall to wall, as in bad golf. The arms and shoulders hold a steady position until the elbow makes its chuck: there are no prior departures preceding the chuck from the elbow. You must learn to stay longer on the right side and stay tighter. The swing will take you, and then your body weight will be added to the swing.

Most golfers will come up on the downswing instead of driving down and going below the original address position. Some will rise two to three inches and settle back after the swing. They refuse to believe that they are guilty of this movement. Some jump and even spin out with their feet. Stay inside your shoes. Stay down on the insteps of your feet.

The mechanics of the body being what they are, the following moves will take place under the conditions to be outlined. If there are any deviations, the cause-and-effect sequence will not take place. Joe has the knowledge of anatomy, so take advantage of it and put forth some effort in order to acquire his swing. Knowledge and application are the first two steps in acquiring the Joe Norwood golf swing.

Stay in your shoes and give the hands and arms full opportunity to function. Letting out the shaft is accomplished by the full extension of the right arm and a maximum move onto the left leg. Staying on the ball longer is a habit with Lee Trevino. A top player will get about twelve to fourteen inches of follow-through after impact with a driver. He will get about six to eight inches with an iron. Joe says, "Abe Mitchell, one of the longest hitters ever, had a follow-through of about eighteen inches with a driver; Snead and Hogan, about fourteen inches." The average golfer has about two inches of follow-through. The easy way to swing is to go around the ball, and the hard way is to acquire the move that will take you down and through the ball. How long is your right side? How long is your right arm? Most golfers are finished with a bent right arm at impact. The loss of power and distance is due to coming to the ball with an unfinished swing, or thrust.

The thrusting right arm becomes fully extended when the elbow is closed to its maximum position and forces the right hand below the original address position. In a full thrust the right hand will go about five to seven inches below the left hand; then and only then will the swing take the body. The right hand goes below the knees, then out and up into that high finish. This is a rather strenuous move, and it will not be made voluntarily; you must make it happen. This is the only way to force the hands into finishing six to eight inches above the head. This is "climbing the wall," a very awkward move, and also a very rewarding one.

Most golfers have the leg action that takes the arms into the swing, but Joe's arm lengthens the leg. The combined action of the arm and shoulder is thrust downward against the holding left arm. When the right wrist gets below the left hand; it will then take the body and legs through the shot, into the crosslateral, and onto the strong, holding left leg. The left knee won't go to the big toe of the left foot unless it is forced to do so.

The right arm is three feet longer on the front part of the swing than it is on the backswing. How long is your right arm before you make the turn with the body? Swing below the knees and add to your extension.

It is easy to do, easy to teach, easy to get the right knee to kick into the swing instead of letting the swing take the leg. Stay on the right side until the swing takes you.

Learn how to take a divot. Drive down below the address position. Don't feel finished at impact. Ninety per cent of players do not use the extensor muscles. The flicking right hand will stop the thrusting action of the arm, and the extensor muscles will never come into play.

Assume the address position on your prop, and extend the left arm and index finger. Set the right hand and forearm at the waist-high position, with the right index finger extended also. Try to touch the left index finger with the right index finger. Note the full extension of the right arm required to do so. A partial extension is a lax move, and a full extension is a dynamic one. Retain the right hand and get the right arm straightened ten inches before impact. The compression at impact will scare you. The instant the arm ceases to extend, the right hand will come into play; the longer the extension, the longer the hand is delayed. The delayed hands will go down and through the shot; otherwise they go around the ball. Arriving at the point of impact with a curve will result in a curve after impact, and the ball will be hooked. The straight line starts at the point of impact and continues to the end of the follow-through on that straight line. The club must be squared to enable it to contact the ball and impart a straight line of flight. There can be no deviations in Position Three in order to bring the squared blade to the point of impact.

On the follow-through, if the hands do not get any higher than the neck, they will detour by going around the neck. The hands must go six to eight inches above the head for the proper follow-through. Hold the left wrist during the follow-through and let the left elbow bend at the top of the swing. You will look like a "Class A" golfer with a high finish.

The shank: The commitment is made in Position Three. The left arm carries to the ball on the downswing. The right arm, which failed to act, or swing, comes to life belatedly and slashes at the ball when the swing is almost past the ball position.

Make the down part of the swing immediately upon reaching the end of the backswing. Don't let the left arm carry toward the ball; keep the right arm active—it should start swinging down at the end of the vertical going up, and not going for a ride with the carrying left arm.

Depth: It is impossible to go too deep in the downswing. The more depth in the downswing merely assures that much more of the front part of the swing, or follow-through, going "down," cannot be overdone. This is where "staying behind the ball and waiting for the clubhead" takes place. Too many golfers make a shallow swipe at the ball. "Go down another foot," says Joe. The pivoting action of the shoulders prevents one from digging into the turf, even though he is driving down. Don't be afraid to drive downward. As the right shoulder goes under, the left rises and so prevents the clubhead from becoming buried in the turf. To get maximum loft "go down another foot."

The pictures of pros showing a rollout on the left foot after impact defies good form. When the pros are lucky enough to get to the ball prior to the rollout, all ends well most of the time. This calls for split-second timing, but they are tempting Fate each and every time, and this helps to keep them on the alert or uptight, as they really can't trust themselves. The element of risk is great in the league they play in; it is an unforgiving game.

Procedures

Practice setting up for each shot in a sequential pattern:

1. Put the blade to the ball with both hands on the shaft.
2. Extend the left arm.
3. Position the right foot for the proper distance from the ball to accommodate the extended left arm.
4. Take the prop position.
5. Complete the grip with the right hand.
6. Lighten the torso.

The Stance for Short Shots

Generally, the stance to be described here is usually for shots under the thirty-yard range but can be made from sixty to ninety yards if so dictated by the circumstances and the player.

The stance for the short shot should begin where the long shot ends. Take a full backswing and make a full extension on the down and finish high with the hands above the head. The leg position is now where you should be in addressing the ball for a short shot in the thirty-yard-or-less range.

Follow a set routine when taking a stance. Always place the clubhead behind the ball first for direction, then place the right foot, which should be straight and parallel to the clubhead. Next, the left foot is placed with the toe pointing out and ahead at a forty-five-degree angle. Take a deep breath and hold it for the duration of the swing. This lightens the torso to the tune of about ten pounds. Now shift the weight over and onto the left leg. About 65 to 75 per cent of the weight should be on the left leg for this position to be properly assumed. The toes are trying to dig in, and the legs are solidly set and affording the torso ample support.

Generally speaking, the best stance for the small shot is open. It permits greater extension of the arms on the follow-through.

This action will help you to assume the stance on the left side a bit easier. Stand up straight with feet together, and place the left foot out at a forty-five-degree angle. Place the right hand on the right hip and give a slight downward and forward push, which has you making a slight curtsy, with the right buttock going down and under. The feeling of getting up on the left leg is from an underneath movement. The left knee travels toward the big toe of the left foot on the inside of the instep. When the weight shift is completed, the left knee must remain studded in that position throughout the entire swing. Accuracy permits no extraneous movement during the swing. About 65 to 75 per cent of the weight is on the left leg at this point. Relax the right knee, letting it drop down and inward. This lowers the right hip, which in turn frees the torso of any tension and allows the arms to travel freely. The right foot is canted inward.

This open stance permits more freedom of movement and does allow the clubhead to stay on the ball longer because the arms are permitted to advance forward farther. With a putter in hand, take a stance with the bulk of the weight on the right leg. Then make a forward putting stroke and measure the distance traveled by the clubhead by making a mark at the point of complete extension. Take the open stance as outlined here and make the same forward putting stroke and you will be amazed at the greater distance the arms were permitted to advance the clubhead.

To review this stance in more detail, review the material on "climbing the wall."

The open stance may be used for varying distances, even to ninety yards. The player's skill, choice of club, and terrain are the variables to be considered.

The Chip Shot and the Pitch-and-run Shot

Take the grip, extend the left arm, place the blade squared for the target, and place the right foot to parallel the blade. Place the left foot forward and out so that the toe is pointing at a forty-five-degree angle. Do not lean forward or sag, but make a weight shift onto the left leg.

Activate the thumb and forefinger, take the clubhead away from the ball in the prescribed manner, and return the clubhead to the ball from the elbow. Here again the elbow goes out toward first base, then continues on the line of flight—it does not cross the line of flight. There is no down in the swing, as the clubhead only goes to about a knee-high position. (There is a down in the swing only when the arms go above the waist.) The clubhead leaves the ball on the backswing and merely returns to the ball from the elbow.

The left arm must hold its extension because this is the guide for the straight line. The toe of the club leaves the ball first, and the return to the ball is made with the heel leading the clubhead.

The basic difference between a chip shot and a pitch-and-run shot is the speed of the clubhead. They are both small shots, with the clubhead going to about a knee-high position on the backswing. The variables encountered will dictate the club to be used as well as the confidence the player may have in any individual club. The mechanics of the stroke are the same for every club. The putting stroke extended classifies these two shots.

Setting the seal of the wrist hoods the clubhead, and swinging from the elbow imparts overspin to the ball. The ball will run on a straight line when it has been struck a downward, pinching blow from a hooded face. The ball runs with topspin, whenever it hits an obstacle it will kick one way or another, but it will always right itself by resuming the straight line again. It is uncanny how straight it will run until it stops. It can run in and out of a dozen ground depressions, and each time it recovers, it resumes its straight line. It rides over stones, pebbles, rough grass, and bare spots. It is always fighting to right itself, just as though it were alive. A deflection is a momentary detour. This proves the built-in action that overspin imparts. A ball hit with an oscillating movement will impart sidespin to the ball, and when it is deflected it will continue on the line of deflection. When it kicks to the left it will continue going to the left, and vice versa. Joe can hit a true running ball across a cinder field and it will run straight, become deflected, and repeat this action time and again. It seems to ride over obstacles, and it never ceases to amaze the onlookers the way the energized ball travels.

The straight line imparted to the ball at impact from a loaded left arm in conjunction with the squared blade is entirely dependable; it will perform each and every time just as it is programmed. Pinpoint accuracy is assured in each and every shot. Nothing but the arms move in making this shot; the body is still, anchored like a ten-ton rock, toes gripping, the posture is erect, and nothing but the arms move.

The choice of club is yours; depending on the lie and distance, you can expect the same result or action from each and every club as long as the mechanics of the swing are maintained.

A chip shot is a putt extended. The clubhead does not rise above the knees.

A chip shot should not be attempted at a distance greater than the length of the green. When made from a distance greater than the length of the green, the ball will run off the green just as an airplane comes in too hot for a short runway.

A green without a sand trap behind it is a safe place to try a pitch-and-run shot.

Thumb and forefinger control will give you the delicate touch needed around the green for the chip and pitch-and-run shots. The holding left arm and wrist will give you an arrow-straight line and enable you to get down in two.

The Pitch Shot

A pitch shot is a half-to-three-quarter swing and can be made from a full swing also. The variables of distance and terrain call for the player's judgment in club selection. Clubhead speed generated will dictate the length of the swing.

The hands will go to waist high or above in this shot, and there will be a down in the returning stroke. A down means that the vertical must be made by chucking from the elbow. The sharper the downstroke is made, the more loft will be attained from the clubhead. Use of the word "sharper" is not intended to mean speed but how close to the point of the backswing the down starts. The sharp blow of the diamond cutter is pictured with this usage. He does not rotate prior to making the downward stroke, nor does he change the plane of the cutting instrument. This fact holds true for every shot the golfer is called upon to make during the course of play or practice. Fortunately, there are only two choices one can make: horizontal or vertical; to swing around the hips or under the hips; right shoulder over or under.

Joe quotes the great Walter Hagen with the following: "You can't win without mastering the chip and pitch shots." Neither can you score well without them.

Sand Shots

"You should not be in them" is about all that Joe has to say about making sand shots out of bunkers. Since there is always a possibility, however slight, a bit about sand shots is offered.

The British style is to dump the ball out of the bunker; the Americans like to blast them out.

Plant the feet solidly, shuffle them until a firm stance is taken, with weight about fifty-fifty on each leg. Swing with the arms only. Lighten the torso, as in all shots. Keep the body quiet and the knees flexed.

Let the sand do the work. To dump the ball out, one must drive the ball "doon" into the sand—yes, down into the sand—and when it lights on the green it will die fast.

When the ball is below the lip of a bunker, drive the ball into the bank. The mind will refuse to accept this action at first. It is a squeeze shot, and the ball will pop up gracefully, and upon landing it will die almost instantly. Don't try to scoop the ball or cut it out with a lifting action. Just drive it into the bank. Open or close the face as the distance dictates.

Hold the left arm and smack the ball with the right arm, keeping the body quiet throughout the action. This applies to either the dump shot or the blast.

The dump shot is less violent than the blast shot, and Joe prefers it.

In shallow traps, where the ball has room to run on the green, one can use a seven-iron, as in making a chip shot.

Again, the lie, distance, and individual choice of club depend upon the physical shape and condition of the trap and the player.

The Lob or Cut or Pizza Shot

The physical mechanics involved in the Joe Norwood golf swing are all identical in all shots and with all of the clubs. The one exception in setting up to make a shot is in the pizza, as Joe loves to call it, more commonly known as the lob or cut shot.

The object of the lob shot is to get the ball airborne quickly and to have it die as quickly as possible after landing on the green.

The stance is open, as it is for all short shots. The grip is the same as it is in all the other shots. The exception is in the left arm. The left arm is not loaded at the address position, as it is in all the other shots. It is set up as it is for the putt, the left wrist being set and sealed, with the elbow opened, or relaxed. The left wrist must be set, and the set, or seal, retained during the stroke. The takeaway is made with the right, as in all other shots.

Properly hit, the ball will rise quickly, and upon landing on the green will bounce and bobble once or twice and then come to almost an instant stop. Improperly hit, the ball will roll more—how much more will depend upon how much you missed making clean contact, or how much you missed making the sharp downward thrust.

The trick or secret in making this shot is in how the downstroke is made. The sharper the downstroke is made the sooner the ball rises, and the sooner it rises, the quicker it will die on the green. Do not rotate with the knees or shoulders, stand steady, and make the first move after reaching the end of the backswing downward; do not carry the club toward the ball. The deeper the downstroke the more rise you will put on the ball. The more rise put on the ball, the more braking power the ball will have on landing on the green —one bounce, one bobble, and a complete stop.

Many advocate making an outside-in swing for the cut shot, but Joe finds it unnecessary. He assumes the normal stance (open, of course), merely lays the blade back, or open, according to the loft and distance required, and makes the shot from inside-out, as in any other shot. He is masterful in making the pizza from various types of terrain and conditions, including hard-pan and cinders. The ball bounces once, bobbles and sputters in its tracks, and stops almost instantly.

Put your faith in the mechanics of Joe's golf-o-metrics, and confidence in shot-making will become yours, to have and to keep always.

The Putt

The term "the old master" applies to Joe in every phase of the golf swing but particularly so when it comes to the putting stroke. This is his specialty. He dearly loves to putt and to chip also.

Until you have seen Joe make a seventy-five-foot downhill putt with about a nine-foot break you just haven't seen anything.

Putting is not an art form and not an individual effort sort of thing where everyone develops what seems to be most effective or comfortable for himself or herself. There is a definite pattern in Joe's putting technique, and it is based on very sound knowledge.

Walter J. Travis, Australian-born American citizen, was the first foreigner to win the British Amateur, in 1904. He played the British Amateur with a center-shafted Schenectady putter borrowed from a friend. This style of putter resembled a croquet mallet. It became popular in Britain after Travis won there; the British were miffed with Walter J. and banned that type of putter in 1909 and finally legalized it in 1952. Travis won the U. S. Amateur in 1900, 1901, and 1903. He was semi-finalist in 1898, 1899, 1906, 1908, and 1914. He also was runner-up in the U. S. Open in 1902. He was a self-taught golfer and started at the age of thirty-four.

Joe says, "The British set the tees way back purposely because Travis was a short hitter and could barely make the distances covering the gorse areas." He certainly could putt, and he certainly did. To this day Walter J. Travis is mentioned with the top putters in the history of golf.

In the book *Walter Hagen,* Bobby Locke writes, "I learned the method of putting largely from Walter Hagen in 1937. The term he used for taking the club back and still keeping it square was that you hooded the face. He proved to me that this backswing applies true topspin to the ball and is in fact the only type of backswing with the putter that will apply true topspin. Hagen, in his heyday, was probably the world's greatest putter, and I was happy to learn from him." Joe states that Hagen learned from the great Walter J. Travis.

Walter J. Travis practiced putting about four hours a day, says Joe. Travis sunk milk bottles into the green and putted for those small openings. A regulation-size cup seemed large by comparison.

Joe played golf with Walter J. Travis in 1913. Travis studied Joe's putting style, and Walter revealed to him what he was doing, but not how to, and this is where Joe had to apply himself and find out the "how to" and "what with."

There are two elements involved in a putt: line and distance. Distance is a matter of individual judgment. Everyone can learn to control the putter blade and stroke the ball on a straight line. Having control of 50 per cent of the putting stroke allows you to concentrate on the other half involved. This will increase your chances of dropping those long ones and more of the short ones. It gives you a 50 per cent edge on the player who is struggling to maintain a straight line and to putt for distance. The line Joe controls is as straight as a yardstick. It can be yours also.

The stance for the putt is the same as for a chip shot, and here too inhaling and holding to lighten the torso are most beneficial.

The left arm need not be fully extended, but the left wrist must be sealed so that there will be no movement between the blade of the putter and the elbow. A straight line must be maintained from the elbow down to the knuckle of the pinky finger. The swing is from the apex of the arm.

Would you believe that about fifty years ago Joe acquired a patent on a device that instantly imparted the Walter J. Travis feeling and technique? The most important effect this induced was to retain a nonmoving shaft. It also removed the oscillating movement of the hands and wrists. Everything must be quiet—the body, the shaft, and, of course, the feet.

The use of the hands will produce a sidespin to the ball, and it will run off-line when deflected and will take the break and magnify the reaction.

Watch the butt of the shaft when making a putting stroke. Does it move back and forth like a pendulum between the wrists? If so, this is a moving shaft. The clubhead should never pass the hands in any shot. When the butt of the shaft moves, the clubhead will pass the hands. A still shaft will allow the hands to remain ahead of the clubhead.

Most golfers are either wrist or arm/shoulder putters, and almost all of them swing up on the ball instead of hitting down on it.

The hand is an oscillator, and very seldom can it repeat the same move. A variation is always introduced, and whatever the blade imparts to the ball, it will react accordingly.

To differentiate: A ball stroked with an oscillating action will have sidespin, whereas a ball stroked with a hooded blade will impart overspin, and it will be what Joe calls a running ball.

Hitting up on the ball is natural for most players. They stand up for the putt instead of down into the insteps of the feet, with the weight shifted over to the left side. A misconception about applying topspin has them hitting up also. A hooded blade hitting down and through pinches the ball and imparts the overspin.

Gripping ever so lightly gives the player absolutely no control. Joe is just as tight in his legs and feet and in his grip for a ten-inch putt as he is for a two-hundred-yard shot.

Nothing is left to chance; everything is set up and locked in and held during the swing—this means for every shot with any club.

The setting of the left hand into a convex position and holding tight with the pinky and wrist will require a certain amount of familiarity, as it will set up a tendency to tighten up through the forearm and even into the shoulder. Trying to swing from the apex is another area one must become familiar with as well as the muscles just mentioned. Remember the learning curve, and rest assured that these parts will soon become second nature. Everything above the elbow can be free and easy, but the straight line from the elbow to the knuckle of the pinky of the left hand must be held in a straight line.

Thirteen clubs have round grips. Why not the fourteenth? Why use an entirely different grip with the fourteenth club? Joe advocates a round grip for the putter. All grips should be alike for all clubs. It will take a very short time to become accustomed to a round grip on a putter. Use it to practice with at the beginning, and it won't be long before it will seem natural. *almost vertical*

Due to the angle of the putter, the wrists are almost vertical in taking the grip. To set the seal of the wrist and to make the forward press are very small moves. The left hand must hold its position when the right hand makes a forward press into the left hand. Do not advance the hands and arms in trying to make the forward press, as this action does not actually hood the face of the club. Should you advance the hands and arms into a forward press it is gone the moment you make the backswing. The forward press and the hooding of the face of the club are made with the grip. The left hand holds while the right wrist makes an over-and-down move, locking or sealing the wrist; only this action will hood the face of the club. Once the seal is set it is never released during the swing.

The seal of the right wrist can be a subtle or sneaky cause of release. The move in the putt is so small that the release goes undetected. The left wrist is double trouble, as it wants to help in the making of the swing, both backward and forward. It is merely a holding unit.

The left wrist is loaded . . . set . . . full of compression. Any release in any of the holding parts will introduce an oscillating action, imparting sidespin to the ball. Any release will result in a slight push or pull in the putting stroke. Most golfers release at or before impact. The grip should be retained for two to three inches beyond impact or two to three seconds after impact. This applies to every shot made.

All parts of the left and right hands and arms are held as a single unit, and the stroke is made with all parts holding as a single unit. The right elbow is the only moving part.

Should a wrinkle on the right wrist make the slightest movement, you can rest assured that the seal of the wrist has been released. The seal is tight at all times. Many pros set themselves up properly and look great on the backswing, but they release on the forward part of the putting stroke. Watch a pro practice putting. He misses to the left or the right, and once in a while he goes straight in. At close range with the help of a 7×50 binocular, watch the wrinkles on the right wrist. It will tell the story of the missed putts. The subtle release will cause one stroke to pull and another one to push, and the ball travels either to the left or to the right. Now and again the pro is mystified with a putt that runs a straight line—it doesn't break as planned, the target is missed; that is one for Walter J. Travis.

When practicing the putting stroke, just watch the ball run true. Don't be concerned with trying to make it drop into the cup. At this point you are trying to discipline the parts that go into the stroke, and that should be your primary goal. Just forget about sinking putts, and soon you will be sinking more putts accidentally than you ever did on purpose. The ball should run without any oscillation.

Practice putting with a range ball. Set the stripe so that it is top and bottom, and after it is stroked it should run with topspin, and all you will see is a single line. When you see a wobbly line or when the line no longer retains a pattern, you will know that somewhere you released a part and introduced an oscillating move.

The best way to practice is to putt against a known break and putt straight for the hole. Again, upon introducing any departures the ball will run off at a break, and when all parts are held, the ball will run true on a straight line, sidehill, downhill, uphill . . . putt straight for the cup. The releases are subtle, and putting against the break is the only sure way of testing as to whether or not the parts were held. The ball will either run true on a straight line or it will run off at the break instead of following the terrain into the cup. When you become attuned to the parts and what is needed to hold them you will, upon impact, know that you have made a successful putt. You will know that the putt made is deadly and going for the cup and most likely into it. The subtle feelings of holding onto all the parts will relay the message of success even prior to impact.

The hands being in a vertical position, you should have the feeling of stroking the ball with the butt of your right wrist.

Stories of unidentified flying objects are usually met with a certain amount of skepticism; but such stories carry a great amount of validity when compared with the next statement. Are you ready for this? Joe never plays a break when he putts. He putts straight for the hole—yes, straight for the hole, whether it be a sidehill or a downhill putt. About a dozen books could be written from all of the objections and theories that would be bounced back after that statement.

The most elementary doubter accuses Joe of being a speed putter. The best objection is that it defies the laws of physics. Joe is not a speed putter, and as a matter of fact there is so much compression in his grip, the ball is hit so solidly and it travels so slowly, it seems as if it won't reach its target, but it goes on and on and on.

The power of the downward stroke plus the weight of the putter head, combined with the hooded blade produce a pinch to the ball that imparts overspin to it. And it will follow the terrain in a true and straight line and will not fall off at the break; it will override it and continue its course, defying the laws of physics. Joe's putt will run true on a cobblestone road.

Use the shaft of another club placed on the ground for a guide to make the backstroke. A yardstick is even better, or scratch a line on the ground. With all parts set and held, the dimple of the right wrist at eleven o'clock; the backward stroke with the putter should take it slightly inside the line, and of course it returns on an inside-out path. Don't lift the putter on the backstroke or cross the line of flight by making an outside-in backstroke. The feelings of taking the toe of the clubhead away and returning the heel are what you should be looking for, and the blade is always squared.

Putting has been relegated to the place where all unsolvable things are cast. It is so mystifying that it is considered to be an art form. How else to categorize it? Experts hesitate to tell anyone that there is more to it than an individual effort learned by trial and error. There are reliable factors that can be definitely depended upon. Touch and feel constitute an individual art form, but certainly not the mechanics of the stroke. Knowledge, application, and feel are everyone's privileges; judgment is the individual factor supplied by the player.

In executing a putting stroke, the swing feeling should be the very same that it is when using any club other than a putter. It shouldn't be a backward push then a forward pull. There is far more rhythm in a swing than in that type of movement. The feeling of holding and swinging is the same as in any other shot. Develop the holding parts and eventually you, too, will own this firm, smooth, and deadly action. The stance is tight, the grip is tight, the elbow is open and the ability to make solid contact with the ball lightly and delicately is now yours. Hold the left and smack it with the right; be bold, hit it for an extra foot; you own a straight line now and it will head right for the cup.

Everything in what Joe Norwood does is keyed to control, and it is most important in the putting stroke, as the margin for error is minimal. The more control one acquires the more fluid, rhythmic, and lighter the stroke becomes. A sticky elbow must be disciplined before it will act "natural." The degree of improving touch and feel is unlimited.

Alpha and Omega

Alpha and omega, the beginning and the end. Make a new beginning through the golf-o-metrics and the end result will be a swing that you can own. Joe says, "If you have a golf swing, you can play with hockey sticks."

Joe admonishes his people to discipline themselves to doing all things in the same way in trying to acquire his golf swing.

"Don't be in a hurry," he is apt to say. To encourage striving, he relates how many years it took him to isolate certain parts. The best advice one can give to an interested golfer is to work on each part in a systematic pattern. Acquire each one and then go on to the next part.

Your swing will reflect and reward an honest effort in adhering to the disciplines as outlined.

To the many disillusioned, those discouraged, skeptics and scoffers: The golf swing is not an ethereal movement. Anyone who has operable joints can learn the mechanics. Verve and skill, of course, are individual contributions and not to be confused with gaining the knowledge that takes the mystery out of the golf swing, nor the ability to make the moves. Whether young or old, male or female, tall or short, lean or fat, everyone without afflictions can give it a big try and manage to become adept at what they are doing simply because of the built-in factors of the body; seven out of ten people, male or female, measure the same in the length of the forearms. They all have elbows and knees that operate the same. They flex, open, and close in identical patterns. Wrists and fingers operate in similar movements in spite of differences in shapes and sizes. Joe can't promise to make a virtuoso out of anyone. But to the extent of individual capabilities one certainly can learn the "musical scale" of the golf swing. Joe's golf-o-metrics will develop the mechanics that will enable one to strike a golf ball with overspin, causing it to fly, or roll, on a straight line. Control is the name of the game in reality. Being able to own, or control, 50 per cent of the two elements, or factors, determining the flight of the ball is great odds by anyone's standards. Distance, the second element, is purely an individual effort. Golf can be fun when the mystery of the swing is reduced to mere facts.